THE YALE SHAKESPEARE

EDITED BY

WILBUR L. CROSS   TUCKER BROOKE

PUBLISHED UNDER THE DIRECTION
OF THE
DEPARTMENT OF ENGLISH, YALE UNIVERSITY,
ON THE FUND
GIVEN TO THE YALE UNIVERSITY PRESS IN 1917
BY THE MEMBERS OF THE
KINGSLEY TRUST ASSOCIATION
(SCROLL AND KEY SOCIETY OF YALE COLLEGE)
TO COMMEMORATE THE SEVENTY-FIFTH ANNIVERSARY
OF THE FOUNDING OF THE SOCIETY

·: *The Yale Shakespeare* :·

PERICLES, PRINCE OF TYRE

EDITED BY

ALFRED R. BELLINGER

LVX ET VERITAS

NEW HAVEN · YALE UNIVERSITY PRESS
LONDON · HUMPHREY MILFORD
OXFORD UNIVERSITY PRESS · MCMXXV

TABLE OF CONTENTS

		Page
The Text	. . . . . .	1
Notes	. . . . . .	93
Appendix A.	Sources of the Play . .	112
Appendix B.	The History of the Play .	116
Appendix C.	Authorship of the Play .	121
Appendix D.	The Text of the Present Edition	129
Appendix E.	Suggestions for Collateral Reading . . .	132
Index of Words Glossed	. . . .	135

The facsimile opposite reproduces the title-page of the Elizabethan Club copy of the first edition of 'Pericles.'

THE LATE, *Scipio Squyer . 5. May 169*

And much admired Play,

Called

Pericles, Prince
of Tyre.

With the true Relation of the whole Historie,
aduentures, and fortunes of the said Prince:

As also,

The no lesse strange, and worthy accidents,
in the Birth and Life, of his Daughter
MARIANA.

As it hath been diuers and sundry times acted by.
his Maiesties Seruants, at the Globe on
the Banck-side..

By William ⬥✦⬥ Shakespeare.

Imprinted at London for *Henry Gosson*, and are
to be sold at the signe of the Sunne in
Pater-noster row, &c.
1 6 0 9.

[DRAMATIS PERSONÆ.

ANTIOCHUS, *King of Antioch.*
PERICLES, *Prince of Tyre.*
HELICANUS, } *two Lords of Tyre.*
ESCANES,
SIMONIDES, *King of Pentapolis.*
CLEON, *Governor of Tarsus.*
LYSIMACHUS, *Governor of Mitylene.*
CERIMON, *a Lord of Ephesus.*
THALIARD, *a Lord of Antioch.*
PHILEMON, *Servant to Cerimon.*
LEONINE, *Servant to Dionyza.*
Marshal.
A Pandar.
BOULT, *his Servant.*

The Daughter of Antiochus.
DIONYZA, *Wife to Cleon.*
THAISA, *Daughter to Simonides.*
MARINA, *Daughter to Pericles and Thaisa.*
LYCHORIDA, *Nurse to Marina.*
A Bawd.

Lords, Ladies, Knights, Gentlemen, Sailors, Pirates,
Fishermen, and Messengers.

DIANA.

GOWER, *as Chorus.*

SCENE: *In various Mediterranean countries.*]

Dramatis Personæ; *cf. n.*

ACT FIRST

Enter Gower.

To sing a song that old was sung,
From ashes ancient Gower is come,
Assuming man's infirmities,
To glad your ear, and please your eyes.   4
It hath been sung at festivals,
On ember-eves, and holy-ales;
And lords and ladies in their lives
Have read it for restoratives: 8
The purchase is to make men glorious;
Et bonum quo antiquius, eo melius.
If you, born in these latter times,
When wit's more ripe, accept my rimes,   12
And that to hear an old man sing
May to your wishes pleasure bring,
I life would wish, and that I might
Waste it for you like taper-light.   16
This Antioch, then, Antiochus the Great
Built up, this city, for his chiefest seat,
The fairest in all Syria,
I tell you what mine authors say.   20
This king unto him took a fere,
Who died and left a female heir,
So buxom, blithe, and full of face
As heaven had lent her all his grace;   24

Act First; *cf. n.*   Enter Gower; *cf. n.*
6 ember-eves; *cf. n.*   holy-ales: *holidays; cf. n.*
9 purchase: *gain*
10 Et bonum quo antiquius, eo melius: *and the more ancient a good
    thing, the better*   17, 18 Cf. *n.*   20 Cf. *n.*
21 fere: *mate*   22, 23 Cf. *n.*   24 heaven: *i.e. God*

With whom the father liking took,
And her to incest did provoke.
Bad child, worse father! to entice his own
To evil should be done by none.   28
By custom what they did begin
Was with long use account no sin.
The beauty of this sinful dame
Made many princes thither frame,   32
To seek her as a bed-fellow,
In marriage-pleasures play-fellow:
Which to prevent, he made a law,
To keep her still, and men in awe,   36
That whoso ask'd her for his wife,
His riddle told not, lost his life:
So for her many a wight did die,
As yon grim looks do testify.   40
What now ensues, to the judgment of your eye
I give, my cause who best can justify.   *Exit.*

Scene One

[*Antioch.   A Room in the Palace*]

Enter Antiochus, Prince Pericles, and Followers.

Ant. Young Prince of Tyre, you have at large
   receiv'd
The danger of the task you undertake.
   Per. I have, Antiochus, and, with a soul
Embolden'd with the glory of her praise,   4
Think death no hazard in this enterprise.   *Music.*
   Ant. Bring in our daughter, clothed like a bride,

25, 26 *Cf. n.*   28 should: *which should*   32 frame: *go*
36 still: *always*   38 told not: *not being guessed*
40 *Cf. n.*   1 Young Prince of Tyre; *cf. n.*   receiv'd: *learned*

For the embracements even of Jove himself;
At whose conception, till Lucina reign'd,   8
Nature this dowry gave, to glad her presence,
The senate-house of planets all did sit,
To knit in her their best perfections.

Enter Antiochus' Daughter.

Per. See, where she comes apparell'd like the
          spring,   12
Graces her subjects, and her thoughts the king
Of every virtue gives renown to men!
Her face the book of praises, where is read
Nothing but curious pleasures, as from thence   16
Sorrow were ever rac'd, and testy wrath
Could never be her mild companion.
You gods, that made me man, and sway in love,
That have inflam'd desire in my breast   20
To taste the fruit of yon celestial tree
Or die in the adventure, be my helps,
As I am son and servant to your will,
To compass such a boundless happiness!   24
    Ant. Prince Pericles,—
    Per. That would be son to great Antiochus.
    Ant. Before thee stands this fair Hesperides,
With golden fruit, but dangerous to be touch'd;   28
For death-like dragons here affright thee hard:
Her face, like heaven, enticeth thee to view
Her countless glory, which desert must gain;
And which, without desert, because thine eye   32
Presumes to reach, all thy whole heap must die.
Yon sometime famous princes, like thyself,

8 Lucina: *the goddess of childbirth*
9 glad her presence: *make her personality glad*
10, 11 *Cf. n.*   13, 14 *Cf. n.*
16 curious: *delicate, particular*   as: *as though*
17 rac'd: *razed, done away with*   27 Hesperides; *cf. n.*

Drawn by report, adventurous by desire,
Tell thee with speechless tongues and semblance
    pale,   36
That without covering, save yon field of stars,
Here they stand martyrs, slain in Cupid's wars;
And with dead cheeks advise thee to desist
For going on death's net, whom none resist.   40
    Per. Antiochus, I thank thee, who hath taught
My frail mortality to know itself,
And by those fearful objects to prepare
This body, like to them, to what I must;   44
For death remember'd should be like a mirror,
Who tells us life's but breath, to trust it error.
I'll make my will then; and as sick men do,
Who know the world, see heaven, but feeling woe, 48
Gripe not at earthly joys as erst they did;
So I bequeath a happy peace to you
And all good men, as every prince should do;
My riches to the earth from whence they came,   52
             [*To the Daughter of Antiochus.*]
But my unspotted fire of love to you.
Thus ready for the way of life or death,
I wait the sharpest blow.
    Ant. Scorning advice, read the conclusion then; 56
Which read and not expounded, 'tis decreed,
As these before thee, thou thyself shalt bleed.
    Daugh. Of all say'd yet, mayst thou prove pros-
    perous!
Of all say'd yet, I wish thee happiness!   60
    Per. Like a bold champion, I assume the lists,
Nor ask advice of any other thought
But faithfulness and courage.

40 For going on: *for fear of going into*
59 Of all say'd yet: *more than all who have assayed yet; cf. n.*

The Riddle

'I am no viper, yet I feed   64
  On mother's flesh which did me breed;
  I sought a husband, in which labour
  I found that kindness in a father.
  He's father, son, and husband mild,   68
  I mother, wife, and yet his child.
  How they may be, and yet in two,
  As you will live, resolve it you.'

Sharp physic is the last: but, O you powers!   72
That give heaven countless eyes to view men's acts,
Why cloud they not their sights perpetually,
If this be true, which makes me pale to read it?
Fair glass of light, I lov'd you, and could still,   76
Were not this glorious casket stor'd with ill:
But I must tell you now my thoughts revolt;
For he's no man on whom perfections wait
That, knowing sin within, will touch the gate.   80
You're a fair viol, and your sense the strings,
Who, finger'd to make man his lawful music,
Would draw heaven down and all the gods to hearken;
But being play'd upon before your time,   84
Hell only danceth at so harsh a chime.
Good sooth, I care not for you.
      Ant. Prince Pericles, touch not, upon thy life,
For that's an article within our law,   88
As dangerous as the rest. Your time's expir'd:
Either expound now or receive your sentence.
      Per. Great king,
Few love to hear the sins they love to act;   92
'Twould braid yourself too near for me to tell it.

64-69 *Cf. n.*   81 sense: *senses*
85 *Cf. n.*   93 braid: *upbraid*

Who has a book of all that monarchs do,

He's more secure to keep it shut than shown;

For vice repeated is like the wandering wind,   96

Blows dust in others' eyes, to spread itself;

And yet the end of all is bought thus dear,

The breath is gone, and the sore eyes see clear

To stop the air would hurt them. The blind mole casts   100

Copp'd hills towards heaven, to tell the earth is throng'd

By man's oppression; and the poor worm doth die for 't.

Kings are earth's gods; in vice their law's their will;

And if Jove stray, who dares say Jove doth ill?   104

It is enough you know; and it is fit,

What being more known grows worse, to smother it.

All love the womb that their first being bred,

Then give my tongue like leave to love my head.   108

    Ant. [*Aside.*] Heaven, that I had thy head! he has found the meaning;

But I will gloze with him. Young Prince of Tyre,

Though by the tenour of our strict edict,

Your exposition misinterpreting,   112

We might proceed to cancel off your days;

Yet hope, succeeding from so fair a tree

As your fair self, doth tune us otherwise:

Forty days longer we do respite you;   116

If by which time our secret be undone,

This mercy shows we'll joy in such a son:

And until then your entertain shall be

96-100 *Cf. n.*
101 Copp'd: *peaked*
103 *Cf. n.*   108 *Cf. n.*
112-115 *Cf. n.*

100 would: *which would*
102 poor worm: *mole*
110 gloze: *use fair words*
119 entertain: *entertainment*

As doth befit our honour and your worth.   120

Manet Pericles solus.

Per. How courtesy would seem to cover sin,
When what is done is like a hypocrite,
The which is good in nothing but in sight!
If it be true that I interpret false,   124
Then were it certain you were not so bad
As with foul incest to abuse your soul;
Where now you're both a father and a son,
By your untimely claspings with your child,—   128
Which pleasure fits a husband, not a father;—
And she an eater of her mother's flesh,
By the defiling of her parent's bed;
And both like serpents are, who though they feed   132
On sweetest flowers, yet they poison breed.
Antioch, farewell! for wisdom sees, those men
Blush not in actions blacker than the night,
Will shun no course to keep them from the light.   136
One sin, I know, another doth provoke;
Murder's as near to lust as flame to smoke.
Poison and treason are the hands of sin,
Ay, and the targets, to put off the shame: 140
Then, lest my life be cropp'd to keep you clear,
By flight I'll shun the danger which I fear.   *Exit.*

Enter Antiochus.

Ant. He hath found the meaning, for which we
    mean
To take his head.   144
He must not live to trumpet forth my infamy,
Nor tell the world Antiochus doth sin
In such a loathed manner;
And therefore instantly this prince must die,   148

135 Blush: *who blush*
140 targets: *shields*   put off: *turn aside*

For by his fall my honour must keep high.
Who attends us there?

Enter Thaliard.

    Thal.   Doth your highness call?
    Ant. Thaliard,
You're of our chamber, and our mind partakes   152
Her private actions to your secrecy;
And for your faithfulness we will advance you.
Thaliard, behold, here's poison, and here's gold;
We hate the Prince of Tyre, and thou must kill
    him: 156
It fits thee not to ask the reason why,
Because we bid it. Say, is it done?
    Thal. My lord, 'tis done.
    Ant. Enough.   160

Enter a Messenger.

Let your breath cool yourself telling your haste.
    Mess. My lord, Prince Pericles is fled.   [*Exit.*]
    Ant.   [*To Thaliard.*] As thou
Wilt live, fly after; and, as an arrow shot
From a well-experienc'd archer hits the mark   164
His eye doth level at, so thou ne'er return
Unless thou say 'Prince Pericles is dead.'
    Thal. My lord,
If I can get him within my pistol's length,   168
I'll make him sure enough: so, farewell to your high-
    ness.
    Ant. Thaliard, adieu!   [*Exit Thaliard.*]
                Till Pericles be dead,
My heart can lend no succour to my head.   *Exit.*

152 partakes: *imparts*
161 telling your haste: *explaining the cause of your haste*
168 length: *range*

Scene Two

[*Tyre. A Room in the Palace*]

Enter Pericles with his Lords.

Per. Let none disturb us.—[*Aside*] Why should
   this change of thoughts,
The sad companion, dull-ey'd melancholy,
Be my so us'd a guest, as not an hour
In the day's glorious walk or peaceful night—   4
The tomb where grief should sleep—can breed me
   quiet?
Here pleasures court mine eyes, and mine eyes shun
   them,
And danger, which I feared, is at Antioch,
Whose arm seems far too short to hit me here;   8
Yet neither pleasure's art can joy my spirits,
Nor yet the other's distance comfort me.
Then it is thus: the passions of the mind,
That have their first conception by mis-dread,   12
Have after-nourishment and life by care;
And what was first but fear what might be done,
Grows elder now and cares it be not done.
And so with me: the great Antiochus,—   16
'Gainst whom I am too little to contend,
Since he's so great can make his will his act,—
Will think me speaking, though I swear to silence;
Nor boots it me to say I honour him,   20
If he suspect I may dishonour him;
And what may make him blush in being known,
He'll stop the course by which it might be known.

Scene Two S. d. Enter Pericles; *cf. n.*
3 us'd: *familiar*   as: *that*
9 joy: *gladden*   15 cares: *takes care*
18 can . . . act: *that he can perform his will*
20 boots it me: *does it avail me*

With hostile forces he'll o'erspread the land, 24
And with the ostent of war will look so huge,
Amazement shall drive courage from the state,
Our men be vanquish'd ere they do resist,
And subjects punish'd that ne'er thought offence: 28
Which care of them, not pity of myself,—
Who am no more but as the tops of trees,
Which fence the roots they grow by and defend
    them,—
Make both my body pine and soul to languish, 32
And punish that before, that he would punish.

Enter [Helicanus and] all the Lords to Pericles.

1. Lord. Joy and all comfort in your sacred breast!
2. Lord. And keep your mind, till you return to us,
Peaceful and comfortable. 36
    Hel. Peace, peace! and give experience tongue.
They do abuse the king that flatter him;
For flattery is the bellows blows up sin;
The thing the which is flatter'd, but a spark, 40
To which that blast gives heat and stronger glowing;
Whereas reproof, obedient and in order,
Fits kings, as they are men, for they may err:
When Signior Sooth here does proclaim a peace, 44
He flatters you, makes war upon your life.
Prince, pardon me, or strike me, if you please;
I cannot be much lower than my knees. *[Kneeling.]*
    Per. All leave us else; but let your cares o'erlook 48
What shipping and what lading's in our haven,
And then return to us. *[Exeunt Lords.]*
                Helicanus, thou
Hast mov'd us; what seest thou in our looks?
    Hel. An angry brow, dread lord. 52

25 ostent: *show*   49 lading: *cargo*

Per. If there be such a dart in prince's frowns,
How durst thy tongue move anger to our face?

Hel. How dare the plants look up to heaven, from
    whence
They have their nourishment?

Per.   Thou know'st I have power 56
To take thy life from thee.

Hel. I have ground the axe myself;
Do you but strike the blow.

Per.   Rise, prithee, rise;
Sit down; thou art no flatterer: 60
I thank thee for it; and heaven forbid
That kings should let their ears hear their faults hid!
Fit counsellor and servant for a prince,
Who by thy wisdom mak'st a prince thy servant,   64
What wouldst thou have me do?

Hel.   To bear with patience
Such griefs as you yourself do lay upon yourself.

Per. Thou speak'st like a physician, Helicanus,
That minister'st a potion unto me   68
That thou wouldst tremble to receive thyself.
Attend me then: I went to Antioch,
Where as thou know'st, against the face of death
I sought the purchase of a glorious beauty,   72
From whence an issue I might propagate
Are arms to princes and bring joys to subjects.
Her face was to mine eye beyond all wonder;
The rest, hark in thine ear, as black as incest;   76
Which by my knowledge found, the sinful father
Seem'd not to strike, but smooth; but thou know'st
    this,
'Tis time to fear when tyrants seem to kiss.

70 Attend: *listen to*   74 Are arms: *such as are arms*
78 smooth: *flatter*

Which fear so grew in me I hither fled,   80
Under the covering of a careful night,
Who seem'd my good protector; and, being here,
Bethought me what was past, what might succeed.
I knew him tyrannous; and tyrants' fears   84
Decrease not, but grow faster than the years.
And should he doubt it, as no doubt he doth,
That I should open to the listening air
How many worthy princes' bloods were shed,   88
To keep his bed of blackness unlaid ope,
To lop that doubt he'll fill this land with arms,
And make pretence of wrong that I have done him;
When all, for mine, if I may call 't, offence,   92
Must feel war's blow, who spares not innocence:
Which love to all, of which thyself art one,
Who now reprov'st me for it,—

    Hel.   Alas! sir.
    Per. Drew sleep out of mine eyes, blood from my
      cheeks,   96
Musings into my mind, with thousand doubts
How I might stop this tempest, ere it came;
And finding little comfort to relieve them,
I thought it princely charity to grieve for them.   100
    Hel. Well, my lord, since you have given me leave
      to speak,
Freely will I speak.   Antiochus you fear,
And justly too, I think, you fear the tyrant,
Who either by public war or private treason   104
Will take away your life.
Therefore, my lord, go travel for a while,
Till that his rage and anger be forgot,
Or till the Destinies do cut his thread of life.   108

83 succeed: *come next*   86 doubt it: *suspect*
89 unlaid ope: *undiscovered*
92 for . . . offence: *for my offence, if I may call it so*

Your rule direct to any; if to me,
Day serves not light more faithful than I'll be.
   Per. I do not doubt thy faith;
But should he wrong my liberties in my absence?   112
   Hel. We'll mingle our bloods together in the earth,
From whence we had our being and our birth.
   Per. Tyre, I now look from thee then, and to Tarsus
Intend my travel, where I'll hear from thee,   116
And by whose letters I'll dispose myself.
The care I had and have of subjects' good
On thee I'll lay, whose wisdom's strength can bear it.
I'll take thy word for faith, not ask thine oath;   120
Who shuns not to break one will sure crack both.
But in our orbs we'll live so round and safe,
That time of both this truth shall ne'er convince,
Thou show'dst a subject's shine, I a true prince.   124
                            Exeunt.

Scene Three

[*The Same. An Antechamber in the Palace*]

Enter Thaliard solus.

   Thal. So this is Tyre, and this the court.
Here must I kill King Pericles; and if I do not, I
am sure to be hanged at home: 'tis dangerous.
Well, I perceive he was a wise fellow, and had   4
good discretion, that, being bid to ask what he
would of the king, desired he might know none
of his secrets: now do I see he had some reason
for it; for if a king bid a man be a villain, he is   8

116 Intend: *turn*   thee: *Helicanus*   122 orbs: *spheres*
123 *Time shall never overcome this truth in us both*
124 shine: *brightness, glory*   4 he was a wise fellow; *cf. n.*

bound by the indenture of his oath to be one.
Hush! here come the lords of Tyre.

Enter Helicanus, Escanes, with other Lords.

Hel. You shall not need, my fellow peers of Tyre,
Further to question me of your king's departure: 12
His seal'd commission, left in trust with me,
Doth speak sufficiently he's gone to travel.
  Thal. [*Aside.*] How! the king gone!
  Hel. If further yet you will be satisfied,   16
Why, as it were unlicens'd of your loves,
He would depart, I'll give some light unto you.
Being at Antioch—
  Thal.   [*Aside.*] What from Antioch?
  Hel. Royal Antiochus—on what cause I know
        not—   20
Took some displeasure at him, at least he judg'd so;
And doubting lest that he had err'd or sinn'd,
To show his sorrow he'd correct himself:
So puts himself unto the shipman's toil,   24
With whom each minute threatens life or death.
  Thal. [*Aside.*] Well, I perceive
I shall not be hang'd now, although I would;
But since he's gone, the king it sure must please: 28
He 'scap'd the land, to perish at the sea.
I'll present myself. [*Aloud.*] Peace to the lords of
        Tyre.
  Hel. Lord Thaliard from Antiochus is welcome.
  Thal. From him I come,   32
With message unto princely Pericles;
But since my landing I have understood
Your lord hath betook himself to unknown travels,

9 indenture: *contract*
17, 18 Why . . . depart: *why he wished to depart without the leave
        of you who love him*   34 *Cf. n.*

My message must return from whence it came.   36
   Hel. We have no reason to desire it,
Commended to our master, not to us:
Yet, ere you shall depart, this we desire,
As friends to Antioch, we may feast in Tyre.   40
                                 Exeunt.

Scene Four

[Tarsus. A Room in the Governor's House]

Enter Cleon the Governor of Tarsus, with [Dionyza]
his wife and others.

   Cle. My Dionyza, shall we rest us here,
And by relating tales of others' griefs,
See if 'twill teach us to forget our own?
   Dio. That were to blow at fire in hope to quench
   it;   4
For who digs hills because they do aspire
Throws down one mountain to cast up a higher.
O my distressed lord! even such our griefs are;
Here they're but felt, and seen with mischief's eyes,   8
But like to groves, being topp'd, they higher rise.
   Cle. O Dionyza,
Who wanteth food, and will not say he wants it,
Or can conceal his hunger till he famish?   12
Our tongues and sorrows do sound deep
Our woes into the air; our eyes do weep
Till tongues fetch breath that may proclaim them
    louder;
That if heaven slumber while their creatures want,   16
They may awake their helps to comfort them.
I'll then discourse our woes, felt several years,

Scene Four Tarsus; *cf. n.*   5 aspire: *mount up*   8, 9 *Cf. n.*

And, wanting breath to speak, help me with tears.
    Dio. I'll do my best, sir.   20
    Cle. This Tarsus, o'er which I have the government,
A city on whom plenty held full hand,
For riches strew'd herself even in the streets;
Whose towers bore heads so high they kiss'd the
      clouds,   24
And the strangers ne'er beheld but wonder'd at;
Whose men and dames so jetted and adorn'd,
Like one another's glass to trim them by:
Their tables were stor'd full to glad the sight,   28
And not so much to feed on as delight;
All poverty was scorn'd, and pride so great,
The name of help grew odious to repeat.
    Dio. O! 'tis too true.   32
    Cle. But see what heaven can do! By this our
      change,
These mouths, whom but of late earth, sea, and air
Were all too little to content and please,
Although they gave their creatures in abundance,   36
As houses are defil'd for want of use,
They are now starv'd for want of exercise;
Those palates who, not yet two summers younger,
Must have inventions to delight the taste,   40
Would now be glad of bread, and beg for it;
Those mothers who, to nousle up their babes,
Thought nought too curious, are ready now
To eat those little darlings whom they lov'd.   44
So sharp are hunger's teeth, that man and wife
Draw lots who first shall die to lengthen life.
Here stands a lord, and there a lady weeping;
Here many sink, yet those which see them fall   48
Have scarce strength left to give them burial.

26 jetted: *walked proudly*   42 nousle: *foster, train up*

Is not this true?

    Dio. Our cheeks and hollow eyes do witness it.

    Cle. O! let those cities that of plenty's cup   **52**

And her prosperities so largely taste,

With their superfluous riots, hear these tears:

The misery of Tarsus may be theirs.

Enter a Lord.

    Lord. Where's the lord governor?   **56**

    Cle. Here.

Speak out thy sorrows which thou bring'st in haste,

For comfort is too far for us to expect.

    Lord. We have descried, upon our neighbouring
        shore,   **60**

A portly sail of ships make hitherward.

    Cle. I thought as much.

One sorrow never comes but brings an heir

That may succeed as his inheritor;   **64**

And so in ours. Some neighbouring nation,

Taking advantage of our misery,

Hath stuff'd these hollow vessels with their power,

To beat us down, the which are down already;   **68**

And make a conquest of unhappy me,

Whereas no glory's got to overcome.

    Lord. That's the least fear; for by the semblance

Of their white flags display'd, they bring us peace, **72**

And come to us as favourers, not as foes.

    Cle. Thou speak'st like him 's untutor'd to repeat:

'Who makes the fairest show means most deceit.'

But bring they what they will and what they can, **76**

What need we fear?

The ground's the lowest and we are half way there.

Go tell their general we attend him here,

---

61 portly : *stately*   70 *Where there is no glory in overcoming*

To know for what he comes, and whence he comes,   80
And what he craves.

   Lord. I go, my lord.   [*Exit.*]

   Cle. Welcome is peace if he on peace consist;
If wars, we are unable to resist.   84

Enter Pericles with Attendants.

   Per. Lord governor, for so we hear you are,
Let not our ships and number of our men,
Be like a beacon fir'd to amaze your eyes.
We have heard your miseries as far as Tyre,   88
And seen the desolation of your streets:
Nor come we to add sorrow to your tears,
But to relieve them of their heavy load;
And these our ships, you happily may think   92
Are like the Troyan horse was stuff'd within
With bloody veins, expecting overthrow,
Are stor'd with corn to make your needy bread,
And give them life whom hunger starv'd half dead. 96

   All. The gods of Greece protect you!
And we'll pray for you.

   Per.   Arise, I pray you, rise:
We do not look for reverence, but for love,
And harbourage for ourself, our ships, and men.   100

   Cle. The which when any shall not gratify,
Or pay you with unthankfulness in thought,
Be it our wives, our children, or ourselves,
The curse of heaven and men succeed their evils! 104
Till when—the which, I hope, shall ne'er be seen—
Your Grace is welcome to our town and us.

   Per. Which welcome we'll accept; feast here awhile,
Until our stars that frown lend us a smile.   108

Exeunt.

83 consist: *insist*   92 happily: *haply, perhaps*
93 the Troyan horse; *cf. n.*   95 *Cf. n.*

ACT SECOND

Enter Gower.

Here have you seen a mighty king
His child, iwis, to incest bring;
A better prince and benign lord,
That will prove awful both in deed and word.   **4**
Be quiet, then, as men should be,
Till he hath pass'd necessity.
I'll show you those in troubles reign,
Losing a mite, a mountain gain.   **8**
The good in conversation,
To whom I give my benison,
Is still at Tarsus, where each man
Thinks all is writ he speken can;   **12**
And, to remember what he does,
Build his statue to make him glorious:
But tidings to the contrary
Are brought your eyes; what need speak **I**?   **16**

Dumb Show.

*Enter at one door Pericles talking with Cleon; all the
Train with them. Enter, at another door, a Gentleman, with a letter to Pericles; Pericles shows the
letter to Cleon; Pericles gives the Messenger a reward, and knights him. Exit Pericles at one door,
and Cleon at another.*

Good Helicane hath stay'd at home,
Not to eat honey like a drone
From others' labours; for though he strive

2 iwis: *certainly, indeed*
9 The good: *i.e. Pericles*   conversation: *behavior*
10 benison: *blessing*   12 writ: *holy writ, Gospel truth*

To killen bad, keep good alive,   20
And to fulfil his prince' desire,
Sends word of all that haps in Tyre:
How Thaliard came full bent with sin
And had intent to murder him;   24
And that in Tarsus was not best
Longer for him to make his rest.
He, doing so, put forth to seas,
Where when men been, there's seldom ease;   28
For now the wind begins to blow;
Thunder above and deeps below
Make such unquiet, that the ship
Should house him safe is wrack'd and split;   32
And he, good prince, having all lost,
By waves from coast to coast is tost.
All perishen of man, of pelf,
Ne aught escapen'd but himself;   36
Till Fortune, tir'd with doing bad,
Threw him ashore, to give him glad;
And here he comes. What shall be next,
Pardon old Gower, this longs the text.   40

                                                     [*Exit.*]

Scene One

[*Pentapolis. An open Place by the Sea-side*]

Enter Pericles wet.

Per. Yet cease your ire, you angry stars of heaven!
Wind, rain, and thunder, remember, earthly man
Is but a substance that must yield to you;
And I, as fits my nature, do obey you.   4

23 full bent with sin: *bent upon sin*
35 All perishen of man: *all the men perish*   pelf: *property*
38 glad: *gladness*   40 longs: *makes too long* (?), *belongs to* (?)
Scene One Pentapolis; *cf. n.*

Alas! the sea hath cast me on the rocks,
Wash'd me from shore to shore, and left my breath
Nothing to think on but ensuing death:
Let it suffice the greatness of your powers   8
To have bereft a prince of all his fortunes;
And having thrown him from your watery grave,
Here to have death in peace is all he'll crave.

Enter three Fishermen.

   1. Fish. What, ho, Pilch!   **12**

   2. Fish. Ha! come and bring away the nets.

   1. Fish. What, Patch-breech, I say!

   3. Fish. What say you, master?

   1. Fish. Look how thou stirrest now! 16
come away, or I'll fetch thee with a wanion.

   3. Fish. Faith, master, I am thinking of
the poor men that were cast away before us
even now.   20

   1. Fish. Alas! poor souls; it grieved my
heart to hear what pitiful cries they made to us
to help them, when, well-a-day, we could scarce
help ourselves.   24

   3. Fish. Nay, master, said not I as much
when I saw the porpoise how he bounced and
tumbled? they say they're half fish, half flesh;
a plague on them! they ne'er come but I look to 28
be washed. Master, I marvel how the fishes live
in the sea.

   1. Fish. Why, as men do a-land; the great
ones eat up the little ones; I can compare our 32
rich misers to nothing so fitly as to a whale;
a' plays and tumbles, driving the poor fry before
him, and at last devours them all at a mouthful.

---

11 S. d. Enter three Fishermen; *cf. n.*   12 Pilch; *cf. n.*
17 with a wanion: *with a vengeance*

Such whales have I heard on o' the land, who 36
never leave gaping till they've swallowed the
whole parish, church, steeple, bells, and all.

Per. [*Aside.*] A pretty moral.

3. Fish. But master, if I had been the 40
sexton, I would have been that day in the
belfry.

2. Fish. Why, man?

3. Fish. Because he should have swal- 44
lowed me too; and when I had been in his
belly, I would have kept such a jangling of the
bells, that he should never have left till he cast
bells, steeple, church, and parish, up again. But 48
if the good King Simonides were of my mind,—

Per. [*Aside.*] Simonides!

3. Fish. We would purge the land of
these drones, that rob the bee of her honey.   52

Per. [*Aside.*] How from the finny subject of the sea
These fishers tell the infirmities of men;
And from their watery empire recollect
All that may men approve or men detect!   56
[*Aloud.*] Peace be at your labour, honest fishermen.

2. Fish. Honest! good fellow, what's that?
if it be a day fits you, search out of the calendar,
and nobody look after it.   60

Per. Y' may see the sea hath cast me on your
coast.

2. Fish. What a drunken knave was the
sea, to cast thee in our way!

Per. A man whom both the waters and the wind, 64
In that vast tennis-court, have made the ball
For them to play upon entreats you pity him;

56 may men approve: *may put men to the test*
58-60 *Cf. n.*   65 tennis-court; *cf. n.*

He asks of you, that never us'd to beg.

   1. Fish. No, friend, cannot you beg? here's 68
them in our country of Greece gets more with
begging than we can do with working.

   2. Fish. Canst thou catch any fishes then?

   Per. I never practised it.   72

   2. Fish. Nay then thou wilt starve, sure;
for here's nothing to be got now-a-days unless
thou canst fish for 't.

   Per. What I have been I have forgot to know,   76
But what I am want teaches me to think on;
A man throng'd up with cold; my veins are chill,
And have no more of life than may suffice
To give my tongue that heat to ask your help;   80
Which if you shall refuse, when I am dead,
For that I am a man, pray you see me buried.

   1. Fish. Die, quoth-a? Now, gods forbid 't!
And I have a gown here; come, put it on; keep 84
thee warm. Now, afore me, a handsome fellow!
Come, thou shalt go home, and we'll have flesh
for all day, fish for fasting-days, and moreo'er
puddings and flap-jacks; and thou shalt be 88
welcome.

   Per. I thank you, sir.

   2. Fish. Hark you, my friend; you said
you could not beg?   92

   Per. I did but crave.

   2. Fish. But crave! Then I'll turn craver
too, and so I shall 'scape whipping.

   Per. Why, are your beggars whipped, 96
then?

   2. Fish. O! not all, my friend, not all; for
if all your beggars were whipped, I would wish

no better office than to be beadle. But, master, 100
I'll go draw up the net.

                     [*Exit with Third Fisherman.*]

Per. How well this honest mirth becomes their
labour!

1. Fish. Hark you, sir; do you know
where ye are?   104

Per. Not well.

1. Fish. Why, I'll tell you: this is called
Pentapolis, and our king the good Simonides.

Per. The good Simonides do you call 108
him?

1. Fish. Ay, sir; and he deserves to be
so called for his peaceable reign and good
government.   112

Per. He is a happy king, since he gains from
his subjects the name of good by his government.
How far is his court distant from this shore?

1. Fish. Marry, sir, half a day's journey; 116
and I'll tell you, he hath a fair daughter, and
to-morrow is her birthday; and there are princes
and knights come from all parts of the world to
joust and tourney for her love.   120

Per. Were my fortunes equal to my desires,
I could wish to make one there.

1. Fish. O! sir, things must be as they
may; and what a man cannot get, he may law- 124
fully deal for—his wife's soul,—

Enter the two Fishermen, drawing up a net.

2. Fish. Help, master, help! here's a fish
hangs in the net, like a poor man's right in the

100 beadle: *a parish officer with power over petty offenders*
120 joust and tourney; *cf. n.*   124, 125 what . . . soul; *cf. n.*

1. Fish. Why, do 'e take it; and the gods
give thee good on 't!

2. Fish. Ay, but hark you, my friend; 'twas 160
we that made up this garment through the rough
seams of the waters; there are certain condolements, certain vails. I hope, sir, if you thrive,
you'll remember from whence you had them.   164

Per. Believe 't, I will.

By your furtherance I am cloth'd in steel;
And spite of all the rupture of the sea,
This jewel holds his building on my arm: 168
Unto thy value will I mount myself
Upon a courser, whose delightful steps
Shall make the gazer joy to see him tread.
Only, my friend, I yet am unprovided   172
Of a pair of bases.

2. Fish. We'll sure provide; thou shalt
have my best gown to make thee a pair, and
I'll bring thee to the court myself.   176

Per. Then honour be but a goal to my will!
This day I'll rise, or else add ill to ill.   [*Exeunt.*]

Scene Two

[*The Same. A public Way. Platform leading to the
Lists. A Pavilion near it, for the reception of the
King, Princess, Ladies, Lords, &c.*]

Enter Simonides, with attendants, and Thaisa.

King. Are the knights ready to begin the triumph?
1. Lord. They are, my liege;

161, 162 made up . . . waters: *brought up through the waves*
163 condolements: *satisfactions for loss*   vails: *gratuities*
167 *In spite of all the sea's destructive power*
168 holds his building: *keeps its place*
169 thy: *the jewel's*   173 bases: *horseman's ornamental skirt*

law; 'twill hardly come out. Ha! bots on 't, '
come at last, and 'tis turned to a rusty armo

Per. An armour, friends! I pray you, let me s
Thanks, Fortune, yet, that after all my crosses
Thou giv'st me somewhat to repair myself;
And though it was mine own, part of my heritage
Which my dead father did bequeath to me,
With this strict charge, even as he left his life,
'Keep it, my Pericles, it hath been a shield
'Twixt me and death';—and pointed to this brace;
'For that it sav'd me, keep it; in like necessity—
The which the gods protect thee from!—it may d
    fend thee.'
It kept where I kept, I so dearly lov'd it;   14
Till the rough seas, that spare not any man,
Took it in rage, though, calm'd, have given 't again.
I thank thee for 't; my shipwrack now's no ill,
Since I have here my father gave in his will.   144

1. Fish. What mean you, sir?

Per. To beg of you, kind friends, this coat of worth,
For it was sometime target to a king;
I know it by this mark. He lov'd me dearly,   148
And for his sake I wish the having of it;
And that you'd guide me to your sovereign's court,
Where with it I may appear a gentleman;
And if that ever my low fortune's better,   152
I'll pay your bounties; till then rest your debtor.

1. Fish. Why, wilt thou tourney for the
lady?

Per. I'll show the virtue I have borne in 156
arms.

128 bots: *a disease of horses;* bots on 't: *an oath on the analogy of
    'plague on it'*   133 And though: *and I thank thee though*
137 brace; *cf. n.*   140 kept: *lived, stayed*
144 my father gave: *what my father gave*   147 target; *cf. n.*
153 pay your bounties: *repay your generosity*

And stay your coming to present themselves.

 King. Return them, we are ready; and our daughter,   4

In honour of whose birth these triumphs are,
Sits here, like beauty's child, whom nature gat
For men to see, and seeing wonder at.

         [Exit a Lord.]

 Thai. It pleaseth you, my royal father, to express 8
My commendations great, whose merit's less.

 King. It's fit it should be so; for princes are
A model, which heaven makes like to itself:
As jewels lose their glory if neglected,   12
So princes their renowns if not respected.
'Tis now your honour, daughter, to explain
The labour of each knight in his device.

 Thai. Which, to preserve mine honour, I'll perform.   16

    The first Knight passes by.

 King. Who is the first that doth prefer himself?
 Thai. A knight of Sparta, my renowned father;
And the device he bears upon his shield
Is a black Ethiop reaching at the sun;   20
The word, *Lux tua vita mihi.*

 King. He loves you well that hold his life of you.

    The Second Knight.

Who is the second that presents himself?

 Thai. A prince of Macedon, my royal father; 24
And the device he bears upon his shield
Is an arm'd knight that's conquer'd by a lady;

---

3 stay: *await*   4 Return them: *announce to them*
14, 15 *Cf. n.*   15 labour: *achievements*
17 prefer: *present*   21 Lux . . . mihi: *Thy light my life*

The motto thus, in Spanish, *Piu por dulzura que por
   fuerza.*

Third Knight.

King. And what's the third?
Thai.   The third of Antioch; 28
And his device, a wreath of chivalry;
The word, *Me pompæ provexit apex.*

Fourth Knight.

King. What is the fourth?
Thai. A burning torch that's turned upside down; 32
The word, *Qui me alit me extinguit.*
   King. Which shows that beauty hath his power and
      will,
Which can as well inflame as it can kill.

Fifth Knight.

Thai. The fifth, an hand environed with clouds,   36
Holding out gold that's by the touchstone tried;
The motto thus, *Sic spectanda fides.*

Sixth Knight [Pericles].

King. And what's
The sixth and last, the which the knight himself   40
With such a graceful courtesy deliver'd?
   Thai. He seems to be a stranger; but his present is
A wither'd branch, that's only green at top;
The motto, *In hac spe vivo.*   44
   King. A pretty moral;
From the dejected state wherein he is,

27 Piu . . . fuerza: *More by sweetness than by force; cf. n.*
30 Me . . . apex: *The crown of glory has drawn me on*
33 Qui . . . extinguit: *Who feeds me extinguishes me*
36 environed with: *surrounded by*   37 touchstone; *cf. n.*
38 Sic . . . fides: *So should faith be tested*
44 In . . . vivo: *In this hope I live*

He hopes by you his fortunes yet may flourish.

  1. Lord. He had need mean better than his outward
    show   48
Can any way speak in his just commend;
For, by his rusty outside he appears
To have practis'd more the whipstock than the lance.

  2. Lord. He well may be a stranger, for he comes 52
To an honour'd triumph strangely furnished.

  3. Lord. And on set purpose let his armour rust
Until this day, to scour it in the dust.

  King. Opinion's but a fool, that makes us scan 56
The outward habit by the inward man.
But stay, the knights are coming; we'll withdraw
Into the gallery.   *[Exeunt.]*
      Great shouts, and all cry, 'The mean knight!'

Scene Three

[The Same. A Hall of State. A Banquet prepared]

Enter the King and Knights from tilting [Thaisa,
    Ladies, Lords, and Attendants].

  King. Knights,
To say you're welcome were superfluous.
To place upon the volume of your deeds,
As in a title-page, your worth in arms,   4
Were more than you expect, or more than's fit,
Since every worth in show commends itself.
Prepare for mirth, for mirth becomes a feast:
You are princes and my guests.   8

  Thai. But you, my knight and guest;
To whom this wreath of victory I give,

49 commend: *commendation*   53 triumph: *public festivity*
54 *He has let his armour rust on purpose*   57 *Cf. n.*
59 S.d. mean: *of undistinguished appearance*

And crown you king of this day's happiness.

    Per. 'Tis more by fortune, lady, than my merit.   12

    King. Call it by what you will, the day is yours;

And here, I hope, is none that envies it.

In framing an artist art hath thus decreed,

To make some good, but others to exceed;   16

And you're her labour'd scholar.   Come, queen o' the
      feast,—

For, daughter, so you are,—here take your place;

Marshal the rest, as they deserve their grace.

    Knights. We are honour'd much by good Simon-
      ides.   20

    King. Your presence glads our days; honour we
      love,

For who hates honour, hates the gods above.

    Marshal. Sir, yonder is your place.

    Per.   Some other is more fit.

    1. Knight. Contend not, sir; for we are gentlemen   24

That neither in our hearts nor outward eyes

Envy the great nor shall the low despise.

    Per. You are right courteous knights.

    King.   Sit, sir; sit.

    Per. By Jove, I wonder, that is king of thoughts,   28

These cates resist me, she but thought upon.

    Thai. [*Aside.*] By Juno, that is queen of marriage,

All viands that I eat do seem unsavoury,

Wishing him my meat. [*Aloud.*] Sure, he's a gallant
      gentleman.   32

    King. He's but a country gentleman;

He has done no more than other knights have done;

He has broken a staff or so; so let it pass.

    Thai. To me he seems like diamond to glass.   36

---

17 And . . . scholar; *cf. n.*   23 Sir . . . place; *cf. n.*
29 *If I but think of her, these delicacies tempt me not; cf. n.*

Per. Yon king's to me like to my father's picture,
Which tells me in that glory once he was;
Had princes sit, like stars, about his throne,
And he the sun for them to reverence.   40
None that beheld him, but like lesser lights
Did vail their crowns to his supremacy;
Where now his son's like a glow-worm in the night,
The which hath fire in darkness, none in light: 44
Whereby I see that Time's the king of men;
He's both their parent, and he is their grave,
And gives them what he will, not what they crave.

    King. What, are you merry, knights?   48
    Knights. Who can be other in this royal presence?
    King. Here, with a cup that's stor'd unto the brim,
As you do love, fill to your mistress' lips,
We drink this health to you.
    Knights.   We thank your Grace. 52
    King. Yet pause awhile;
Yon knight doth sit too melancholy,
As if the entertainment in our court
Had not a show might countervail his worth.   56
Note it not you, Thaisa?
    Thai.   What is it
To me, my father?
    King.   O, attend, my daughter:
Princes in this should live like gods above,
Who freely give to every one that comes   60
To honour them;
And princes not doing so are like to gnats,
Which make a sound, but kill'd are wonder'd at.
Therefore to make his entrance more sweet,   64
Here say we drink this standing-bowl of wine to him.

56 countervail: *equal*   62, 63 *Cf. n.*
64 entrance: *joining in our festivity*
65 standing-bowl: *bowl with a standard*

Thai. Alas! my father, it befits not me
Unto a stranger knight to be so bold;
He may my proffer take for an offence, 68
Since men take women's gifts for impudence.
 King. How!
Do as I bid you, or you'll move me else.
  Thai. [*Aside.*] Now, by the gods, he could not
   please me better. 72
  King. And further tell him, we desire to know of
   him,
Of whence he is, his name, and parentage.
 Thai. The king, my father, sir, has drunk to you.
 Per. I thank him. 76
 Thai. Wishing it so much blood unto your life.
 Per. I thank both him and you, and pledge him
  freely.
 Thai. And further he desires to know of you,
Of whence you are, your name and parentage. 80
 Per. A gentleman of Tyre, my name, Pericles;
My education been in arts and arms;
Who, looking for adventures in the world,
Was by the rough seas reft of ships and men, 84
And after shipwreck, driven upon this shore.
  Thai. He thanks your Grace; names himself **Peri-
  cles,**
A gentleman of **Tyre,**
Who only by misfortune of the seas 88
Bereft of ships and men, cast on this shore.
 King. Now, by the gods, I pity his misfortune,
And will awake him from his melancholy.
Come, gentlemen, we sit too long on trifles, 92
And waste the time which looks for other revels.

71 move: *anger*   81-85 *Cf. n.*
82 been: *has been*   92 on: *ot*

Even in your armours, as you are address'd,
Will well become a soldier's dance.
I will not have excuse with saying this,   96
'Loud music is too harsh for ladies' heads,'
Since they love men in arms as well as beds.

                                    They dance.

So this was well ask'd, 'twas so well perform'd.
Come, sir;   100
Here's a lady that wants breathing too:
And I have heard, you knights of Tyre
Are excellent in making ladies trip,
And that their measures are as excellent.   104

 Per. In those that practise them they are, my lord.
 King. Oh! that's as much as you would be denied
Of your fair courtesy.   *They dance.*

                    Unclasp, unclasp;
Thanks, gentlemen, to all; all have done well,   108
[*To Pericles.*] But you the best. Pages and lights, to
    conduct
These knights unto their several lodgings! Yours, sir,
We have given order be next our own.

 Per. I am at your Grace's pleasure.   112

 [*King.*] Princes, it is too late to talk of love,
And that's the mark I know you level at;
Therefore each one betake him to his rest;
To-morrow all for speeding do their best.   116

                                    [*Exeunt.*]

94 address'd: *dressed*   95 Will: *You will*
97 Loud music: *the clash of their armor*
99 So this was well ask'd: *I did well to ask this*
101 breathing: *exercising*
106, 107 *Cf. n.*
114 level: *aim*   116 *To-morrow let all do their best at wooing*

Scene Four

[*Tyre.   A Room in the Governor's House*]

Enter Helicanus and Escanes.

Hel. No, Escanes, know this of me,
Antiochus from incest liv'd not free;
For which, the most high gods not minding longer
To withhold the vengeance that they had in store,   4
Due to this heinous capital offence,
Even in the height and pride of all his glory,
When he was seated in a chariot
Of an inestimable value, and his daughter with him,   8
A fire from heaven came and shrivell'd up
Their bodies, even to loathing; for they so stunk,
That all those eyes ador'd them ere their fall
Scorn now their hand should give them burial.   12

Esca. 'Twas very strange.

Hel.   And yet but justice; for though
This king were great, his greatness was no guard
To bar heaven's shaft, but sin had his reward.

Esca. 'Tis very true.   16

Enter two or three Lords.

1. Lord. See, not a man in private conference
Or council has respect with him but he.

2. Lord. It shall no longer grieve without reproof.

3. Lord. And curst be he that will not second it.   20

1. Lord. Follow me then. Lord Helicane, a word.

Hel. With me? and welcome. Happy day, my lords.

1. Lord. Know that our griefs are risen to the top,
And now at length they overflow their banks.   24

3 minding: *being minded*   9, 10 *Cf. n.*
11 ador'd: *which adored*

Hel. Your griefs! for what? wrong not your prince
    you love.
  1. Lord. Wrong not yourself then, noble Helicane;
But if the prince do live, let us salute him,
Or know what ground's made happy by his breath. 28
If in the world he live, we'll seek him out;
If in his grave he rest, we'll find him there;
And be resolv'd he lives to govern us,
Or dead, give's cause to mourn his funeral,   82
And leave us to our free election.
  2. Lord. Whose death's indeed the strongest in our
    censure:
And knowing this kingdom is without a head,
(Like goodly buildings left without a roof   36
Soon fall to ruin) your noble self,
That best know how to rule and how to reign,
We thus submit unto, our sovereign.
  Omnes. Live, noble Helicane!   40
  Hel. Try honour's cause, forbear your suffrages:
If that you love Prince Pericles, forbear.
Take I your wish, I leap into the seas,
Where's hourly trouble for a minute's ease.   44
A twelvemonth longer let me entreat you
To forbear the absence of your king;
If in which time expir'd he not return,
I shall with aged patience bear your yoke.   48
But if I cannot win you to this love,
Go search like nobles, like noble subjects,
And in your search spend your adventurous worth;
Whom if you find, and win unto return,   52
You shall like diamonds sit about his crown.

25 you: *whom you*   31-33 *Cf. n.*
34 strongest . . . censure: *most likely in our opinion*
36 Like: *as*   43 Take I: *if I take*
46 forbear: *bear in patience*

    1. Lord. To wisdom he's a fool that will not yield;
And since Lord Helicane enjoineth us,
We with our travels will endeavour.   56
    Hel. Then you love us, we you, and we'll clasp
    hands:
When peers thus knit, a kingdom ever stands.

                                 [Exeunt.]

Scene Five

[Pentapolis.   A Room in the Palace]

*Enter the King reading of a letter at one door;
the Knights meet him.*

    1. Knight. Good morrow to the good Simonides.
    King. Knights, from my daughter this I let you
    know,
That for this twelvemonth she'll not undertake
A married life.   4
Her reason to herself is only known,
Which yet from her by no means can I get.
    1. Knight. May we not get access to her, my lord?
    King. Faith, by no means; she hath so strictly tied 8
Her to her chamber that 'tis impossible.
One twelve moons more she'll wear Diana's livery;
This by the eye of Cynthia hath she vow'd,
And on her virgin honour will not break it.   12
    3. Knight. Loath to bid farewell, we take our leaves.
                         [Exeunt Knights.]
    King. So,
They are well dispatch'd; now to my daughter's letter.
She tells me here, she'll wed the stranger knight, 16
Or never more to view nor day nor light.

54 *He's a fool who will not yield to wisdom*   3, 4 *Cf. n.*
10, 11 *Cf. n.*

'Tis well, mistress; your choice agrees with mine;
I like that well: nay, how absolute she's in 't,
Not minding whether I dislike or no! 20
Well, I do commend her choice;
And will no longer have it be delay'd.
Soft! here he comes: I must dissemble it.

Enter Pericles.

Per. All fortune to the good Simonides! 24
 King. To you as much! Sir, I am beholding to you
For your sweet music this last night: I do
Protest my ears were never better fed
With such delightful pleasing harmony 28
 Per. It is your Grace's pleasure to commend,
Not my desert.
 King.   Sir, you are music's master.
 Per. The worst of all her scholars, my good lord.
 King Let me ask you one thing. 32
What do you think of my daughter, sir?
 Per. A most virtuous princess.
 King. And she is fair too, is she not?
 Per. As a fair day in summer; wondrous fair. 36
 King. Sir, my daughter thinks very well of you;
Ay, so well that you must be her master,
And she will be your scholar: therefore look to it.
 Per. I am unworthy for her schoolmaster. 40
 King. She thinks not so; peruse this writing else.
 Per. [*Aside.*] What's here?
A letter that she loves the knight of Tyre!
'Tis the king's subtilty to have my life. 44
Oh, seek not to entrap me, gracious lord,
A stranger and distressed gentleman,
That never aim'd so high to love your daughter,

25 beholding: *indebted* 28 *Cf. n.* 44 subtilty: *crafty plot*

But bent all offices to honour her.   48

 King. Thou hast bewitch'd my daughter, and thou
  art
A villain.

 Per. By the gods, I have not:
Never did thought of mine levy offence;   52
Nor never did my actions yet commence
A deed might gain her love or your displeasure.

 King. Traitor, thou liest.

 Per.   Traitor!

 King.   Ay, traitor.

 Per. Even in his throat, unless it be the king,   56
That calls me traitor, I return the lie.

 King. [*Aside.*] Now, by the gods, I do applaud his
  courage.

 Per. My actions are as noble as my thoughts,
That never relish'd of a base descent.   60
I came unto your court for honour's cause,
And not to be a rebel to her state;
And he that otherwise accounts of me,
This sword shall prove he's honour's enemy.   64

 King. No?
Here comes my daughter, she can witness it.

Enter Thaisa.

 Per. Then, as you are as virtuous as fair,
Resolve your angry father, if my tongue   68
Did e'er solicit, or my hand subscribe
To any syllable that made love to you.

 Thai. Why, sir, say if you had,
Who takes offence at that would make me glad?   72

 King. Yea, mistress, are you so peremptory?—

48 bent all offices: *directed all his endeavors*   52 levy: *aim at*
60 relish'd: *had a taste*   68 Resolve: *inform*
73 peremptory: *determined*

I am glad on 't, with all my heart.   *Aside.*
[*Aloud.*] I'll tame you; I'll bring you in subjection.
Will you, not having my consent,   76
Bestow your love and your affections
Upon a stranger?—who, for aught I know,
May be, nor can I think the contrary,
As great in blood as I myself.—   *Aside.* 80
[*Aloud.*] Therefore, hear you, mistress; either frame
Your will to mine; and you, sir, hear you,
Either be rul'd by me, or I'll make you—
Man and wife: 84
Nay, come, your hands and lips must seal it too;
And being join'd, I'll thus your hopes destroy;
And for further grief,—God give you joy!
What! are you both pleas'd?
    Thai.   Yes, if you love me, sir. 88
    Per. Even as my life, my blood that fosters it.
    King. What! are you both agreed?
    Ambo. Yes, if 't please your majesty.
    King. It pleaseth me so well, that I will see you
        wed;   92
And then with what haste you can get you to bed.
                                              Exeunt.

ACT THIRD

Enter Gower.

Now sleep yslacked hath the rout;
No din but snores the house about,
Made louder by the o'erfed breast
Of this most pompous marriage-feast.   4
The cat, with eyne of burning coal,

91 Ambo: *both*   93 *Cf. n.*
1 yslacked hath the rout: *hath quieted the company*   5 eyne: *eyes*

Now couches fore the mouse's hole;
And crickets sing at the oven's mouth,
Are the blither for their drouth.   8
Hymen hath brought the bride to bed,
Where, by the loss of maidenhead,
A babe is moulded.   Be attent;
And time that is so briefly spent   12
With your fine fancies quaintly eche;
What's dumb in show I'll plain with speech.

[*Dumb Show.*]

Enter Pericles and Simonides, at one door with At-
tendants; a Messenger meets them, kneels, and gives
Pericles a letter: Pericles shows it Simonides; the
Lords kneel to Pericles.   Then enter Thaisa with
child, with Lychorida a nurse: the King shows her
the letter; she rejoices: she and Pericles take leave
of her father, and depart.

By many a dern and painful perch,
Of Pericles the careful search   16
By the four opposing coigns,
Which the world together joins,
Is made with all due diligence
That horse and sail and high expense   20
Can stead the quest.   At last from Tyre,—
Fame answering the most strange inquire—
To the court of King Simonides
Are letters brought, the tenour these: 24
Antiochus and his daughter dead;
The men of Tyrus on the head
Of Helicanus would set on

6 fore: *before*   8 *And are the more blithe for their dryness*
13 eche: *eke out*   15-19 *Cf. n.*
22 *Report answering the most widespread inquiry*   21 stead: *help*

The crown of Tyre, but he will none:　28
The mutiny he there hastes t' oppress;
Says to 'em, if King Pericles
Come not home in twice six moons,
He, obedient to their dooms,　32
Will take the crown.　The sum of this,
Brought hither to Pentapolis,
Yravished the regions round,
And every one with claps can sound,　36
'Our heir-apparent is a king!
Who dream'd, who thought of such a thing?'
Brief, he must hence depart to Tyre:
His queen, with child, makes her desire,—　40
Which who shall cross?—along to go.
Omit we all their dole and woe:
Lychorida, her nurse, she takes,
And so to sea.　Their vessel shakes　44
On Neptune's billow; half the flood
Hath their keel cut: but Fortune's mood
Varies again; the grisled north
Disgorges such a tempest forth,　48
That, as a duck for life that dives,
So up and down the poor ship drives.
The lady shrieks, and, well-a-near!
Does fall in travail with her fear;　52
And what ensues in this fell storm
Shall for itself itself perform.
I nill relate, action may
Conveniently the rest convey,　56
Which might not what by me is told.
In your imagination hold

32 dooms: *judgments*　　　　35 Yravished: *delighted*
36 can: *'gan, began to*
45 half . . . cut: *they have made half the voyage*
51 well-a-near!: *well-a-day!*　　　　53 fell: *fierce*
55 nill: *will not; cf. n.*　　　55-57 action . . . told; *cf. n.*

This stage the ship, upon whose deck
The seas-toss'd Pericles appears to speak.   60

[*Exit.*]

Scene One

Enter Pericles, a-shipboard.

Per. The God of this great vast rebuke these surges,
Which wash both heaven and hell; and thou, that hast
Upon the winds command, bind them in brass,
Having call'd them from the deep. O, still   4
Thy deafening, dreadful thunders; gently quench
Thy nimble, sulphurous flashes. O, how, Lychorida,
How does my queen?   Thou storm, venomously
Wilt thou spit all thyself?   The seaman's whistle   8
Is as a whisper in the ears of death,
Unheard.   Lychorida! Lucina, O
Divinest patroness, and midwife gentle
To those that cry by night, convey thy deity   12
Aboard our dancing boat; make swift the pangs
Of my queen's travails!

Enter Lychorida [with an Infant].

Now, Lychorida!

Lyc. Here is a thing too young for such a place,
Who, if it had conceit, would die, as I   16
Am like to do: take in your arms this piece
Of your dead queen.

Per.   How, how, Lychorida?

Lyc. Patience, good sir; do not assist the storm.
Here's all that is left living of your queen,   20
A little daughter: for the sake of it,
Be manly, and take comfort.

Scene One; *cf. n.*   1 rebuke these surges; *cf. n.*
16 conceit: *understanding*

Per.   O you gods!
Why do you make us love your goodly gifts,
And snatch them straight away? We here below   24
Recall not what we give, and therein may
Vie honour with you.
  Lyc.   Patience, good sir,
Even for this charge.
  Per.   Now, mild may be thy life!
For a more blusterous birth had never babe: 28
Quiet and gentle thy conditions! for
Thou art the rudeliest welcome to this world
That e'er was prince's child. Happy what follows!
Thou hast as chiding a nativity   32
As fire, air, water, earth, and heaven can make,
To herald thee from the womb; even at the first
Thy loss is more than can thy portage quit,
With all thou canst find here. Now, the good gods   36
Throw their best eyes upon 't!

Enter two Sailors.

  1. Sail. What courage, sir? God save you!
  Per. Courage enough. I do not fear the flaw;
It hath done to me the worst. Yet for the love   40
Of this poor infant, this fresh new seafarer,
I would it would be quiet.
    1. Sail. Slack the bolins there! thou wilt
not, wilt thou? Blow, and split thyself.   44
    2. Sail. But sea-room, and the brine and
cloudy billow kiss the moon, I care not.
    1. Sail. Sir, your queen must overboard:

24-26 We . . . you; *cf. n.*
27 Even . . . charge: *for the sake of the baby*
35 can . . . quit: *thy safe delivery can atone for*
39 flaw: *squall*   43 bolins: *bowlines*
45 But sea-room and: *only give us sea-room, and though*
46 cloudy billow: *waves like clouds*
                                    47 *Cf. n.*

the sea works high, the wind is loud, and will 48
not lie till the ship be cleared of the dead.

Per. That's your superstition.

1. Sail. Pardon us, sir; with us at sea it
hath been still observed, and we are strong in 52
custom. Therefore briefly yield her, for she
must overboard straight.

Per. As you think meet. Most wretched queen!

Lyc. Here she lies, sir. 56

Per. A terrible child-bed hast thou had, my dear;
No light, no fire: th' unfriendly elements
Forgot thee utterly; nor have I time
To give thee hallow'd to thy grave, but straight 60
Must cast thee, scarcely coffin'd, in the ooze;
Where, for a monument upon thy bones,
And aye-remaining lamps, the belching whale
And humming water must o'erwhelm thy corpse, 64
Lying with simple shells! O Lychorida!
Bid Nestor bring me spices, ink and paper,
My casket and my jewels; and bid Nicander
Bring me the satin coffer: lay the babe 68
Upon the pillow. Hie thee, whiles I say
A priestly farewell to her: suddenly, woman.

[*Exit Lychorida.*]

2. Sail. Sir, we have a chest beneath the
hatches, caulk'd and bitumed ready. 72

Per. I thank thee. Mariner, say what coast
is this?

2. Sail. We are near Tarsus.

Per. Thither, gentle mariner, 76
Alter thy course for Tyre. When canst thou reach it?

2. Sail. By break of day, if the wind cease.

---

70 suddenly: *swiftly*   72 bitumed: *pitched*
77 thy . . . Tyre: *your present course towards Tyre*

Per. O! make for Tarsus.
There will I visit Cleon, for the babe   80
Cannot hold out to Tyrus; there I'll leave it
At careful nursing. Go thy ways, good mariner;
I'll bring the body presently.

                    Exit [followed by Sailors].

Scene Two

[Ephesus. A Room in Cerimon's House]

*Enter Lord Cerimon, with a Servant [and some
        Persons who have been shipwrecked].*

Cer. Philemon, ho!

                    Enter Philemon.

Phil. Doth my lord call?
Cer. Get fire and meat for these poor men;
'T has been a turbulent and stormy night.   4
Ser. I have been in many; but such a night as this
Till now I ne'er endur'd.
Cer. Your master will be dead ere you return;
There's nothing can be minister'd to nature   8
That can recover him. [*To Philemon.*] Give this to
    the 'pothecary,
And tell me how it works.

                    [*Exeunt all except Cerimon.*]

            Enter two Gentlemen.

1. Gent.   Good morrow.
2. Gent. Good morrow to your lordship.
Cer.   Gentlemen,
Why do you stir so early?   12

82 At . . . nursing: *to be carefully nursed*
Scene Two Ephesus; *cf. n.*

    1. Gent. Sir,
Our lodgings, standing bleak upon the sea,
Shook as the earth did quake;
The very principals did seem to rend,   16
And all to topple.   Pure surprise and fear
Made me to quit the house.
    2. Gent. That is the cause we trouble you so early;
'Tis not our husbandry.
    Cer.   O, you say well.   20
    1. Gent. But I much marvel that your lordship,
      having
Rich tire about you, should at these early hours
Shake off the golden slumber of repose.
'Tis most strange,   24
Nature should be so conversant with pain,
Being thereto not compell'd.
    Cer.   I hold it ever,
Virtue and cunning were endowments greater
Than nobleness and riches; careless heirs   28
May the two latter darken and expend,
But immortality attends the former,
Making a man a god.   'Tis known I ever
Have studied physic, through which secret art,   32
By turning o'er authorities, I have—
Together with my practice—made familiar
To me and to my aid the blest infusions
That dwells in vegetives, in metals, stones;   36
And can speak of the disturbances
That nature works, and of her cures; which doth
    give me
A more content in course of true delight
Than to be thirsty after tottering honour,   40

16 principals: *frame-work*   20 husbandry: *thrifty habits*
22 tire: *bed furnishings*   32 physic: *the art of healing*
35 aid: *assistant; cf. n.*

Or tie my treasure up in silken bags,
To please the fool and death.

 2. Gent. Your honour has through Ephesus pour'd
  forth
Your charity, and hundreds call themselves   44
Your creatures, who by you have been restor'd:
And not your knowledge, your personal pain, but even
Your purse, still open, hath built Lord Cerimon
Such strong renown as time shall never decay.   48

  Enter two or three [Servants] with a chest.

 Serv. So; lift there.
 Cer.   What's that?
 Serv.   Sir, even now
Did the sea toss up upon our shore this chest:
'Tis of some wrack.
 Cer.   Set it down; let's look upon 't.
 2. Gent. 'Tis like a coffin, sir.
 Cer.   Whate'er it be, 52
'Tis wondrous heavy. Wrench it open straight;
If the sea's stomach be o'ercharg'd with gold,
'Tis a good constraint of fortune it belches upon us.
 2. Gent. 'Tis so, my lord.
 Cer.   How close 'tis caulk'd and bottomed! 56
Did the sea cast it up?
 Serv. I never saw so huge a billow, sir,
As toss'd it upon shore.
 Cer.   Wrench it open.
Soft! it smells most sweetly in my sense.   60
 2. Gent. A delicate odour.
 Cer. As ever hit my nostril. So, up with it.
O you most potent gods! what's here? a corse!
 2. Gent. Most strange!   64

46 pain: *care*   63 corse: *corpse*

Cer. Shrouded in cloth of state; balm'd and en-
    treasur'd
With full bags of spices! A passport too!
Apollo, perfect me in the characters!
    'Here I give to understand,   68
    If e'er this coffin drives a-land,
    I, King Pericles, have lost
    This queen worth all our mundane cost.
    Who finds her, give her burying;   72
    She was the daughter of a king:
    Besides this treasure for a fee,
    The gods requite his charity!'
If thou liv'st, Pericles, thou hast a heart   76
That even cracks for woe! This chanc'd to-night.
    2. Gent. Most likely, sir.
    Cer.   Nay, certainly to-night;
For look, how fresh she looks. They were too rough
That threw her in the sea. Make a fire within;   80
Fetch hither all my boxes in my closet.
                          [*Exit Second Servant.*]
Death may usurp on nature many hours,
And yet the fire of life kindle again
The o'erpress'd spirits. I heard of an Egyptian,   84
That had nine hours lien dead,
Who was by good appliance recovered.

             Enter one with napkins and fire.

Well said, well said; the fire and cloths.
The rough and woeful music that we have,   88
Cause it to sound, beseech you.
The viol once more;—how thou stirr'st, thou block!

65 entreasur'd: *stored up*
67 *Apollo, enable me to read the writing*
77 to-night: *last night*   82 usurp: *encroach*
84 o'erpress'd: *overcome*   85 lien: *lain*

The music there! I pray you, give her air.
Gentlemen,   92
This queen will live; nature awakes, a warmth
Breathes out of her; she hath not been entranc'd
Above five hours. See how she 'gins to blow
Into life's flower again.

 1. Gent.   The heavens   96
Through you increase our wonder and sets up
Your fame for ever.

 Cer.   She is alive! behold,
Her eyelids, cases to those heavenly jewels
Which Pericles hath lost,   100
Begin to part their fringes of bright gold;
The diamonds of a most praised water
Doth appear, to make the world twice rich. Live,
And make us weep to hear your fate, fair creature, 104
Rare as you seem to be!   *She moves.*

 Thai.   O dear Diana!
Where am I? Where's my lord? What world is this?

 2. Gent. Is not this strange?

 1. Gent.   Most rare.

 Cer.   Hush, my gentle neighbours!
Lend me your hands; to the next chamber bear her. 108
Get linen; now this matter must be look'd to,
For her relapse is mortal. Come, come;
And Æsculapius guide us!
    They carry her away. Exeunt omnes.

97 sets; *cf. n.*   103 twice rich; *cf. n.*
105, 106 *Cf. n.*   110 is mortal: *would be fatal*
111 Æsculapius: *god of healing*

Scene Three

[*Tarsus. A Room in Cleon's House*]

Enter Pericles, at Tarsus, with Cleon and Dionyza [and Lychorida, carrying the infant Marina].

Per. Most honour'd Cleon, I must needs be gone;
My twelve months are expir'd, and Tyrus stands
In a litigious peace. You and your lady
Take from my heart all thankfulness; the gods   4
Make up the rest upon you!

   Cle. Your shakes of fortune, though they haunt you
     mortally,
Yet glance full wanderingly on us.

   Dion.   O your sweet queen!
That the strict fates had pleas'd you had brought her
     hither,   8
To have bless'd mine eyes with her!

   Per.   We cannot but obey
The powers above us. Could I rage and roar
As doth the sea she lies in, yet the end
Must be as 'tis. My gentle babe Marina—whom,   12
For she was born at sea, I have nam'd so—here
I charge your charity withal, leaving her
The infant of your care, beseeching you
To give her princely training, that she may be   16
Manner'd as she is born.

   Cle.   Fear not, my lord, but think
Your Grace, that fed my country with your corn—
For which the people's prayers still fall upon you—
Must in your child be thought on. If neglection   20
Should therein make me vile, the common body,

3 litigious: *questionable*   5 upon: *to*
6-7 *Cf. n.*
20 neglection: *neglect*   7 full wanderingly: *wide of their mark*
                        21 the common body: *the citizens*

By you reliev'd, would force me to my duty;
But if to that my nature need a spur,
The gods revenge it upon me and mine,   24
To the end of generation!
   Per.   I believe you;
Your honour and your goodness teach me to 't,
Without your vows.   Till she be married, madam,
By bright Diana, whom we honour, all   28
Unscissor'd shall this hair of mine remain,
Though I show ill in 't.   So I take my leave.
Good madam, make me blessed in your care
In bringing up my child.
   Dion.   I have one myself,   32
Who shall not be more dear to my respect
Than yours, my lord.
   Per.   Madam, my thanks and prayers.
   Cle. We'll bring your Grace e'en to the edge o'
      the shore;
Then give you up to the mask'd Neptune and   36
The gentlest winds of heaven.
   Per.   I will embrace
Your offer.   Come, dearest madam.   O! no tears,
Lychorida, no tears:
Look to your little mistress, on whose grace   40
You may depend hereafter.   Come, my lord.
                          [Exeunt.]

33 respect: *care*
36 mask'd Neptune: *the mighty sea appearing calm*

Scene Four

[*Ephesus.   A Room in Cerimon's House*]

Enter Cerimon and Thaisa.

Cer. Madam, this letter, and some certain jewels,
Lay with you in your coffer; which are
At your command. Know you the character?
    Thai. It is my lord's.   4
That I was shipp'd at sea, I well remember,
Even on my eaning time; but whether there
Deliver'd, by the holy gods,
I cannot rightly say.   But since King Pericles,   8
My wedded lord, I ne'er shall see again,
A vestal livery will I take me to,
And never more have joy.
    Cer. Madam, if this you purpose as ye speak,   12
Diana's temple is not distant far,
Where you may abide till your date expire.
Moreover, if you please, a niece of mine
Shall there attend you.   16
    Thai. My recompense is thanks, that's all;
Yet my good will is great, though the gift small.
                  Exit [*with Cerimon*].

ACT FOURTH

Enter Gower.

Imagine Pericles arriv'd at Tyre,
Welcom'd and settled to his own desire.
His woeful queen we leave at Ephesus,
Unto Diana there a votaress.   4

---

6 eaning time: *time of bringing forth*   9 *Cf. n.*
10 vestal livery; *cf. n.*   14 your date expire: *you die*

Now to Marina bend your mind,
Whom our fast-growing scene must find
At Tarsus, and by Cleon train'd
In music, letters; who hath gain'd   8
Of education all the grace,
Which makes her both the heart and place
Of general wonder.   But, alack!
That monster envy, oft the wrack   12
Of earned praise, Marina's life
Seeks to take off by treason's knife.
And in this kind hath our Cleon
One daughter, and a wench full grown,   16
Even ripe for marriage-rite; this maid
Hight Philoten, and it is said
For certain in our story, she
Would ever with Marina be: 20
Be 't when she weav'd the sleided silk
With fingers, long, small, white as milk,
Or when she would with sharp needle wound
The cambric, which she made more sound   24
By hurting it; wʰ ᵆn to the lute
She sung, and made the night-bird mute,
That still records with moan; or when
She would with rich and constant pen   28
Vail to her mistress Dian; still
This Philoten contends in skill
With absolute Marina: so
With the dove of Paphos might the crow   32
Vie feathers white.   Marina gets
All praises, which are paid as debts,
And not as given.   This so darks

10 heart and place: *the very center*   18 Hight: *named*
21 sleided: *raw*   26 night-bird: *nightingale*
27 records: *sings*   29 Vail: *do homage*
31 absolute: *perfect*   32 the dove of Paphos; *cf. n.*
34, 35 All . . . given; *cf. n.*   35 darks: *obscures*

In Philoten all graceful marks,   36
That Cleon's wife, with envy rare,
A present murderer does prepare
For good Marina, that her daughter
Might stand peerless by this slaughter.   40
The sooner her vile thoughts to stead,
Lychorida, our nurse, is dead:
And cursed Dionyza hath
The pregnant instrument of wrath   44
Prest for this blow. The unborn event
I do commend to your content:
Only I carried winged time
Post on the lame feet of my rime;   48
Which never could I so convey,
Unless your thoughts went on my way.
Dionyza doth appear,
With Leonine, a murtherer.   *Exit.*

Scene One

[Tarsus.   An open Place near the Sea-shore]

Enter Dionyza, with Leonine.

Dion. Thy oath remember; thou hast sworn to do 't:
'Tis but a blow, which never shall be known.
Thou canst not do a thing i' the world so soon,
To yield thee so much profit. Let not conscience,   4
Which is but cold, inflaming love i' thy bosom,
Inflame too nicely; nor let pity, which
Even women have cast off, melt thee, but be
A soldier to thy purpose.   8
   Leon. I'll do 't; but yet she is a goodly creature.

36 *All attention to the grace of Philoten*   44 pregnant: *ready*
45 Prest: *prepared*   47-50 *Cf. n.*   6 nicely: *scrupulously*

Dion. The fitter, then, the gods should have her.
   Here
She comes weeping for her only mistress' death.
Thou art resolv'd?
   Leon.   I am resolv'd.   12

Enter Marina, with a basket of flowers.

Mar. No, I will rob Tellus of her weed,
To strew thy green with flowers; the yellows, blues,
The purple violets, and marigolds,
Shall as a carpet hang upon thy grave,   16
While summer days doth last. Ay me! poor maid,
Born in a tempest, when my mother died,
This world to me is a lasting storm,
Whirring me from my friends.   20
   Dion. How now, Marina! why do you keep alone?
How chance my daughter is not with you? Do not
Consume your blood with sorrowing; you have
A nurse of me. Lord! how your favour's chang'd   24
With this unprofitable woe. Come,
Give me your flowers, ere the sea mar it.
Walk with Leonine; the air is quick there,
And it pierces and sharpens the stomach. Come,   28
Leonine, take her by the arm, walk with her.
   Mar. No, I pray you;
I'll not bereave you of your servant.
   Dion.   Come, come;
I love the king your father, and yourself,   32
With more than forcign heart. We every day
Expect him here; when he shall come and find
Our paragon to all reports thus blasted,

13 Tellus: *Earth*   14 green: *grave*
20 Whirring: *hurrying*   22 How chance: *how comes it*
24 of: *in*   favour: *face*   26 it: *them*
27 quick: *invigorating*   28 stomach: *spirits*
35 to all reports: *equal to all reports*

He will repent the breadth of his great voyage;   36
Blame both my lord and me, that we have taken
No care to your best courses. Go, I pray you;
Walk, and be cheerful once again; reserve
That excellent complexion, which did steal   40
The eyes of young and old. Care not for me;
I can go home alone.

   Mar.   Well, I will go;
But yet I have no desire to it.

   Dion. Come, come, I know 'tis good for you.   44
Walk half an hour, Leonine, at least.
Remember what I have said.

   Leon.   I warrant you, madam.

   Dion. I'll leave you, my sweet lady, for a while;
Pray you walk softly, do not heat your blood: 48
What! I must have care of you.

   Mar.   My thanks, sweet madam.

                          [*Exit Dionyza.*]
Is this wind westerly that blows?

   Leon.   South-west.

   Mar. When I was born, the wind was north.

   Leon.   Was 't so?

   Mar. My father, as nurse said, did never fear,   52
But cried 'Good seamen!' to the sailors, galling
His kingly hands haling ropes;
And, clasping to the mast, endur'd a sea
That almost burst the deck.   56

   Leon. When was this?

   Mar. When I was born:
Never were waves nor wind more violent;
And from the ladder-tackle washes off   60
A canvas-climber. 'Ha!' says one, 'wilt out?'

38 courses: *interests*   48 softly: *slowly*
54 haling: *pulling*   61 canvas-climber: *seaman*

And with a dropping industry they skip
From stem to stern; the boatswain whistles, and
The master calls, and trebles their confusion.   64
   Leon. Come; say your prayers.
   Mar. What mean you?
   Leon If you require a little space for prayer,
I grant it. Pray; but be not tedious,   68
For the gods are quick of ear, and I am sworn
To do my work with haste.
   Mar.   Why will you kill me?
   Leon. To satisfy my lady.
   Mar. Why would she have me kill'd?   72
Now, as I can remember, by my troth,
I never did her hurt in all my life.
I never spake bad word, nor did ill turn
To any living creature; believe me, la,   76
I never kill'd a mouse, nor hurt a fly;
I trod upon a worm against my will,
But I wept for it. How have I offended,
Wherein my death might yield her any profit,   80
Or my life imply her any danger?
   Leon. My commission
Is not to reason of the deed, but do 't.
   Mar. You will not do 't for all the world, I hope. 84
You are well favour'd, and your looks foreshow
You have a gentle heart. I saw you lately,
When you caught hurt in parting two that fought;
Good sooth, it show'd well in you; do so now;   88
Your lady seeks my life; come you between,
And save poor me, the weaker.
   Leon.   I am sworn,
And will dispatch.

62 dropping: *dripping wet*   85 **well favour'd:** *handsome*

Enter Pirates.

1. Pirate. Hold, villain !   92
                    [*Leonine runs away.*]

2. Pirate. A prize ! a prize !

3. Pirate. Half-part, mates, half-part.

Come, let's have her aboard suddenly.
                    Exit [*Marina, carried by Pirates*].

Enter Leonine.

Leon. These roguing thieves serve the great pirate
        Valdes ;   96

And they have seiz'd Marina.   Let her go ;

There's no hope she'll return.   I'll swear she's dead,

And thrown into the sea.   But I'll see further ;

Perhaps they will but please themselves upon her, 100

Not carry her aboard.   If she remain,

Whom they have ravish'd must by me be slain.   *Exit.*

Scene Two

[*Mitylene.   A Room in a Brothel*]

Enter the three Bawds [*i.e. Pandar, Bawd,
                    and Boult*].

Pand. Boult.

Boult. Sir ?

Pand. Search the market narrowly ; Mitylene
is full of gallants ; we lost too much money this 4
mart by being too wenchless.

    Bawd. We were never so much out of crea-
tures.   We have but poor three, and they can

94 Half-part: *I demand my share*   96 Valdes; *cf. n.*
Scene Two Mitylene; *cf. n.*   5 mart: *market time*

do no more than they can do; and they with 8
continual action are even as good as rotten.

Pand. Therefore, let's have fresh ones, what-
e'er we pay for them.   If there be not a conscience to be used in every trade, we shall never 12
prosper.

Bawd. Thou sayst true; 'tis not the bringing
up of poor bastards, as, I think, I have brought
up some eleven—   16

Boult. Ay, to eleven; and brought them down
again.   But shall I search the market?

Bawd. What else, man?   The stuff we have
a strong wind will blow it to pieces, they are 20
so pitifully sodden.

Pand. Thou sayst true; they're too unwhole-
some, o' conscience.   The poor Transylvanian is
dead, that lay with the little baggage.   24

Boult. Ay, she quickly pooped him; she made
him roast-meat for worms.   But I'll go search
the market.   *Exit.*

Pand. Three or four thousand chequins were 28
as pretty a proportion to live quietly, and so
give over.

Bawd. Why to give over, I pray you? is it a
shame to get when we are old?   32

Pand. O! our credit comes not in like the
commodity, nor the commodity wages not with
the danger; therefore, if in our youths we could
pick up some pretty estate, 'twere not amiss to 36
keep our door hatched.   Besides, the sore terms
we stand upon with the gods will be strong with
us for giving over.

25 pooped: *deceived*   28 chequins: *sequins, gold coins*
30 give over: *give up (the life)*   34 wages not: *is not equal*
37 hatched; *cf. n.*

Bawd. Come, other sorts offend as well as we. 40

Pand. As well as we! ay, and better too; we offend worse. Neither is our profession any trade; it's no calling. But here comes Boult.

Enter Boult, with the Pirates and Marina.

Boult. Come your ways. My masters, you 44 say she's a virgin?

1. Pirate. O, sir, we doubt it not.

Boult. Master, I have gone through for this piece, you see: if you like her, so; if not, I have 48 lost my earnest.

Bawd. Boult, has she any qualities?

Boult. She has a good face, speaks well, and has excellent good clothes; there's no farther 52 necessity of qualities can make her be refused.

Bawd. What's her price, Boult?

Boult. I cannot be bated one doit of a thousand pieces.   56

Pand. Well, follow me, my masters, you shall have your money presently. Wife, take her in; instruct her what she has to do, that she may not be raw in her entertainment.   60

[*Exeunt Pandar and Pirates.*]

Bawd. Boult, take you the marks of her, the colour of her hair, complexion, height, age, with warrant of her virginity; and cry, 'He that will give most, shall have her first.' Such a maiden- 64 head were no cheap thing, if men were as they have been. Get this done as I command you.

43 S. d. Enter Boult, etc.; *cf. n.*
47 gone through: *struck a bargain*   49 earnest: *advance payment*
55 bated one doit: *reduced a farthing*
60 raw: *unskilled*   entertainment: *occupation*

  Boult. Performance shall follow.   *Exit.* 68
 Mar. Alack, that Leonine was so slack, so slow!
He should have struck, not spoke; or that these
  pirates—
Not enough barbarous—had not o'erboard thrown me
For to seek my mother!   72
 Bawd. Why lament you, pretty one?
 Mar. That I am pretty.
 Bawd. Come, the gods have done their part in you.
 Mar. I accuse them not.   76
 Bawd. You are lit into my hands, where you
are like to live.
 Mar. The more my fault
To 'scape his hands where I was like to die. 80
 Bawd. Ay, and you shall live in pleasure.
 Mar. No.
 Bawd. Yes, indeed, shall you, and taste gen-
tlemen of all fashions. You shall fare well; you 84
shall have the difference of all complexions.
What! do you stop your ears?
 Mar. Are you a woman?
 Bawd. What would you have me be, an I be 88
not a woman?
 Mar. An honest woman, or not a woman.
 Bawd. Marry, whip thee, gosling; I think I
shall have something to do with you. Come, 92
you are a young foolish sapling, and must be
bowed as I would have you.
 Mar. The gods defend me!
 Bawd. If it please the gods to defend you by 96
men, then men must comfort you, men must
feed you, men must stir you up. Boult's returned.

[Re-enter Boult.]

Now, sir, hast thou cried her through the 100
market?

Boult. I have cried her almost to the number of her hairs; I have drawn her picture with
my voice.   104

Bawd. And I prithee, tell me, how dost thou
find the inclination of the people, especially of
the younger sort?

Boult. Faith, they listened to me, as they 108
would have hearkened to their father's testa-
ment. There was a Spaniard's mouth so watered,
that he went to bed to her very description.

Bawd. We shall have him here to-morrow 112
with his best ruff on.

Boult. To-night, to-night. But, mistress, do
you know the French knight that cowers i' the
hams?   116

Bawd. Who? Monsieur Veroles?

Boult. Ay, he; he offered to cut a caper at the
proclamation; but he made a groan at it, and
swore he would see her to-morrow.   120

Bawd. Well, well; as for him, he brought his
disease hither: here he does but repair it. I
know he will come in our shadow, to scatter his
crowns in the sun.   124

Boult. Well, if we had of every nation a tra-
veller, we should lodge them with this sign.

Bawd. *[To Marina.]* Pray you, come hither
awhile. You have fortunes coming upon you. 128
Mark me: you must seem to do that fear-
fully, which you commit willingly; to de-

126 sign: *inn sign, Marina*

spise profit where you have most gain.   To
weep that you live as ye do makes pity in 132
your lovers; seldom but that pity begets
you a good opinion, and that opinion a mere
profit.

Mar. I understand you not.   136

Boult. O! take her home, mistress, take her
home; these blushes of hers must be quenched
with some present practice.

Bawd. Thou sayst true, i' faith, so they must; 140
for your bride goes to that with shame which is
her way to go with warrant.

Boult. Faith, some do, and some do not.   But,
mistress, if I have bargained for the joint,— 144

Bawd. Thou mayst cut a morsel off the spit.

Boult. I may so?

Bawd. Who should deny it?   Come, young
one, I like the manner of your garments well. 148

Boult. Ay, by my faith, they shall not be
changed yet.

Bawd. Boult, spend thou that in the town;
report what a sojourner we have; you'll lose 152
nothing by custom.   When nature framed this
piece, she meant thee a good turn; therefore
say what a paragon she is, and thou hast the
harvest out of thine own report.   156

Boult. I warrant you, mistress, thunder shall
not so awake the beds of eels as my giving out
her beauty stir up the lewdly-inclined.   I'll bring
home some to-night.   160

Bawd. Come your ways; follow me.

Mar. If fires be hot, knives sharp, or waters deep,

134 mere: *sure*
141 which . . . warrant: *the way which she is entitled to go*

Untied I still my virgin knot will keep.
Diana, aid my purpose!   164
 Bawd. What have we to do with Diana?
Pray you, will you go with us?   *Exeunt.*

Scene Three

[*Tarsus.   A Room in Cleon's House*]

Enter Cleon and Dionyza.

 Dion. Why, are you foolish?   Can it be undone?
 Cle. O Dionyza! such a piece of slaughter
The sun and moon ne'er look'd upon.
 Dion.   I think
You'll turn a child again.   4
 Cle. Were I chief lord of all this spacious world,
I'd give it to undo the deed.   O lady!
Much less in blood than virtue, yet a princess
To equal any single crown o' the earth   8
I' the justice of compare.   O villain Leonine!
Whom thou hast poison'd too;
If thou hadst drunk to him 't had been a kindness
Becoming well thy fact; what canst thou say   12
When noble Pericles shall demand his child?
 Dion. That she is dead.   Nurses are not the fates,
To foster it, nor ever to preserve.
She died at night; I'll say so.   Who can cross it? 16
Unless you play the pious innocent,
And for an honest attribute cry out
'She died by foul play.'
 Cle.   O! go to.   Well, well,
Of all the faults beneath the heavens, the gods   20

<hr>

Scene Three; *cf. n.*   9 I' . . . compare: *by just comparison*
11 drunk to: *toasted (in poison)*   12 fact: *misdeed*
16 cross: *deny*   18 attribute: *reputation*

Do like this worst.

  Dion.   Be one of those that think
The pretty wrens of Tarsus will fly hence,
And open this to Pericles. I do shame
To think of what a noble strain you are,   24
And of how coward a spirit.

  Cle.   To such proceeding
Who ever but his approbation added,
Though not his prime consent, he did not flow
From honourable sources.

  Dion.   Be it so, then;   28
Yet none does know but you how she came dead,
Nor none can know, Leonine being gone.
She did distain my child, and stood between
Her and her fortunes; none would look on her,   32
But cast their gazes on Marina's face,
Whilst ours was blurted at and held a malkin
Not worth the time of day. It pierc'd me thorough;
And though you call my course unnatural,   36
You not your child well loving, yet I find
It greets me as an enterprise of kindness
Perform'd to your sole daughter.

  Cle.   Heavens forgive it!

  Dion. And as for Pericles,   40
What should he say? We wept after her hearse,
And even yet we mourn; her monument
Is almost finish'd, and her epitaphs
In glittering golden characters express   44
A general praise to her, and care in us
At whose expense 'tis done.

---

23 open: *reveal*
25-28 To . . . sources: *whoever could approve such a crime, though
  not party to it, must be base* 31 distain: *put a stain upon*
34 blurted: *mocked* malkin: *slattern*
35 the time of day: *a civil greeting* thorough: *through*
38 greets: *gratifies*

Cle.   Thou art like the harpy,
Which, to betray, dost, with thine angel's face,
Seize with thine eagle's talons.   48

   Dion. You are like one that superstitiously
Do swear to the gods that winter kills the flies;
But yet I know you'll do as I advise.   [*Exeunt.*]

Scene Four

[*Before the Monument of Marina at Tarsus*]

[*Enter Gower.*]

Gower. Thus time we waste, and long leagues make
      short;
Sail seas in cockles, have, an wish but for 't;
Making—to take your imagination—
From bourn to bourn, region to region.   4
By you being pardon'd, we commit no crime
To use one language in each several clime
Where our scenes seem to live.   I do beseech you
To learn of me, who stand i' the gaps to teach you,   8
The stages of our story.   Pericles
Is now again thwarting the wayward seas,
Attended on by many a lord and knight,
To see his daughter, all his life's delight.   12
Old Helicanus goes along.   Behind
Is left to govern it, you bear in mind,
Old Escanes, whom Helicanus late
Advanc'd in time to great and high estate.   16
Well-sailing ships and bounteous winds have brought
This king to Tarsus, think his pilot thought,

46 harpy; *cf. n.*   49, 50 *Cf. n.*   1 waste: *do away with*
2 have, an wish but for 't: *have what we but wish for*
4 bourn: *boundary*
18 think his pilot thought: *imagine your thought is his pilot*

So with his steerage shall your thoughts grow on,
To fetch his daughter home, who first is gone.   20
Like motes and shadows see them move awhile;
Your ears unto your eyes I'll reconcile.

[*Dumb Show.*]

Enter Pericles at one door with all his Train; Cleon
  and Dionyza at the other.   Cleon shows Pericles the
  tomb; whereat Pericles makes lamentation, puts on
  sackcloth, and in a mighty passion departs. [Exeunt
  Cleon and Dionyza.]

Gower. See how belief may suffer by foul show!
This borrow'd passion stands for true old woe;   24
And Pericles, in sorrow all devour'd,
With sighs shot through, and biggest tears o'er-
      shower'd,
Leaves Tarsus and again embarks.   He swears
Never to wash his face, nor cut his hairs;   28
He puts on sackcloth, and to sea.   He bears
A tempest, which his mortal vessel tears,
And yet he rides it out.   Now please you wit
The epitaph is for Marina writ   32
By wicked Dionyza.
        [*Reads inscription on Marina's monument.*]

The fairest, sweet'st, and best lies here,
Who wither'd in her spring of year:
She was of Tyrus the king's daughter,   36
On whom foul death hath made this slaughter.
Marina was she call'd; and at her birth,
Thetis, being proud, swallow'd some part o' th' earth:

19 steerage: *voyage*
30 tempest: *storm of mental anguish*   his . . . vessel: *the*
    vessel of his life   39 Thetis: *goddess of the sea*

Therefore the earth, fearing to be o'erflow'd,   40
Hath Thetis' birth-child on the heavens bestow'd:
Wherefore she does, and swears she'll never stint,
Make raging battery upon shores of flint.

No visor does become black villainy   44
So well as soft and tender flattery.
Let Pericles believe his daughter's dead,
And bear his courses to be ordered
By Lady Fortune; while our scene must play   48
His daughter's woe and heavy well-a-day
In her unholy service.   Patience then,
And think you now are all in Mitylen.   *Exit.*

Scene Five

[Mitylene.   A Street before the Brothel]

Enter two Gentlemen.

1. Gent. Did you ever hear the like?

2. Gent. No, nor never shall do in such a
place as this, she being once gone.

1. Gent. But to have divinity preached 4
there! did you ever dream of such a thing?

2. Gent. No, no. Come, I am for no more
bawdy-houses. Shall's go hear the vestals sing?

1. Gent. I'll do anything now that is 8
virtuous; but I am out of the road of rutting
forever.   *Exeunt.*

42 stint: *cease*

Scene Six

[The Same.　A Room in the Brothel]

Enter the three Bawds.

Pand. Well, I had rather than twice the worth of her she had ne'er come here.

Bawd. Fie, fie upon her! she is able to freeze the god Priapus, and undo a whole generation; 4 we must either get her ravished, or be rid of her. When she should do for clients her fitment, and do me the kindness of our profession, she has me her quirks, her reasons, her master-reasons, her 8 prayers, her knees; that she would make a puritan of the devil if he should cheapen a kiss of her.

Boult. Faith, I must ravish her, or she'll disfurnish us of all our cavaliers, and make all 12 our swearers priests.

Pand. Now, the pox upon her green-sickness for me!

Bawd. Faith, there's no way to be rid on 't 16 but by the way to the pox. Here comes the Lord Lysimachus, disguised.

Boult. We should have both lord and lown if the peevish baggage would but give way to 20 customers.

Enter Lysimachus.

Lys. How now! How a dozen of virginities?

Bawd. Now, the gods to-bless your honour!

Boult. I am glad to see your honour in good 24 health.

---

4 Priapus: *the god of fertility and generation*	6 fitment: *duty*
7 has me: *has, forsooth*	8 quirks: *subtle arguments, quibbles*
10 cheapen: *bargain for*	14 green-sickness: *anæmia*
19 lown: *loon, menial*	23 to-bless: *bless entirely*

Lys. You may so; 'tis the better for you that your resorters stand upon sound legs. How now, wholesome iniquity! have you that a man 28 may deal withal, and defy the surgeon?

Bawd. We have here one, sir, if she would— but there never came her like in Mitylene.

Lys. If she'd do the deeds of darkness, thou 32 wouldst say.

Bawd. Your honour knows what 'tis to say well enough.

Lys. Well; call forth, call forth.   36

Boult. For flesh and blood, sir, white and red, you shall see a rose; and she were a rose indeed if she had but—

Lys. What, prithee?   40

Boult. O! sir, I can be modest.

Lys. That dignifies the renown of a bawd no less than it gives a good report to a number to be chaste.   [*Exit Boult.*] 44

Bawd. Here comes that which grows to the stalk; never plucked yet, I can assure you.—

[*Enter Boult with Marina.*]

Is she not a fair creature?

Lys. Faith, she would serve after a long 48 voyage at sea. Well, there's for you; leave us.

Bawd. I beseech your honour, give me leave; a word, and I'll have done presently.

Lys. I beseech you, do.   52

Bawd. [*To Marina.*] First, I would have you note, this is an honourable man.

Mar. I desire to find him so, that I may worthily note him.   56

43, 44 report . . . to be chaste: *reputation of being chaste*

Bawd. Next, he's the governor of this country, and a man whom I am bound to.

Mar. If he govern the country, you are bound
to him indeed; but how honourable he is in that 60
I know not.

Bawd. Pray you, without any more virginal
fencing, will you use him kindly?   He will line
your apron with gold.   64

Mar. What he will do graciously, I will
thankfully receive.

Lys. Ha' you done?

Bawd. My lord, she's not paced yet; you 68
must take some pains to work her to your
manage.   Come, we will leave his honour and
her together.

Lys. Go thy ways. [*Exeunt Bawd and Pandar.* 72
Boult retires to the door.] Now, pretty one, how
long have you been at this trade?

Mar. What trade, sir?

Lys. Why, I cannot name 't but I shall offend. 76

Mar. I cannot be offended with my trade.
Please you to name it.

Lys. How long have you been of this pro-
fession?   80

Mar. E'er since I can remember.

Lys. Did you go to 't so young?   Were you a
gamester at five or at seven?

Mar. Earlier too, sir, if now I be one.   84

Lys. Why, the house you dwell in proclaims
you to be a creature of sale.

Mar. Do you know this house to be a place
of such resort, and will come into 't?   I hear say 88

68 paced: *trained*   70 manage: *control*
76 but . . . offend: *without offense*

you are of honourable parts, and are the governor of this place.

 Lys. Why, hath your principal made known
unto you who I am?   92

 Mar. Who is my principal?

 Lys. Why, your herb-woman; she that sets
seeds and roots of shame and iniquity. O! you
have heard something of my power, and so stand 96
aloof for more serious wooing. But I protest to
thee, pretty one, my authority shall not see thee,
or else look friendly upon thee. Come, bring me
to some private place; come, come.   100

 Mar. If you were born to honour, show it now;
If put upon you, make the judgment good
That thought you worthy of it.

 Lys. How's this? how's this? Some more; be
  sage.   104

 Mar. For me,
That am a maid, though most ungentle fortune
Hath plac'd me in this sty, where, since I came,
Diseases have been sold dearer than physic, 108
O that the gods
Would set me free from this unhallow'd place,
Though they did change me to the meanest bird
That flies i' the purer air!

 Lys.   I did not think 112
Thou couldst have spoke so well; ne'er dream'd thou
  couldst.
Had I brought hither a corrupted mind,
Thy speech had alter'd it. Hold, here's gold for thee;
Persever in that clear way thou goest,   116
And the gods strengthen thee!

89 parts: *qualities*
102 If put upon you: *if honor was bestowed upon you (and not
 inherited)*

Mar. The good gods preserve you!

Lys. For me, be you thoughten

That I came with no ill intent, for to me   120

The very doors and windows savour vilely.

Farewell. Thou art a piece of virtue, and

I doubt not but thy training hath been noble.

Hold, here's more gold for thee.   124

A curse upon him, die he like a thief,

That robs thee of thy goodness! If thou dost

Hear from me, it shall be for thy good.

    Boult. [*Advancing.*] I beseech your honour, 128
one piece for me.

    Lys. Avaunt! thou damned door-keeper. Your
house,

But for this virgin that doth prop it, would

Sink and overwhelm you. Away!   [*Exit.*] 132

    Boult. How's this? We must take another
course with you. If your peevish chastity,
which is not worth a breakfast in the cheapest
country under the cope, shall undo a whole 136
household, let me be gelded like a spaniel.
Come your ways.

    Mar. Whither would you have me?

    Boult. I must have your maidenhead taken 140
off, or the common hangman shall execute it.
Come your ways. We'll have no more gentlemen driven away. Come your ways, I say.

Enter Bawd.

    Bawd. How now! what's the matter?   144

    Boult. Worse and worse, mistress; she has
here spoken holy words to the Lord Lysimachus.

119 be you thoughten: *think*
122 piece of virtue: *virtuous creature*   136 cope: *firmament*

Bawd. O! abominable.　　　　　　　　　　　148

Boult. She makes our profession as it were to stink afore the face of the gods.

Bawd. Marry, hang her up forever!

Boult. The nobleman would have dealt with 152 her like a nobleman, and she sent him away as cold as a snowball; saying his prayers too.

Bawd. Boult, take her away; use her at thy pleasure; crack the glass of her virginity, and 156 make the rest malleable.

Boult. An if she were a thornier piece of ground than she is, she shall be ploughed.

Mar. Hark, hark, you gods!　　　　　　　160

Bawd. She conjures; away with her! Would she had never come within my doors! Marry, hang you! She's born to undo us. Will you not go the way of womenkind? Marry, come up, 164 my dish of chastity with rosemary and bays!

[*Exit.*]

Boult. Come, mistress; come your ways with me.

Mar. Whither wilt thou have me?

Boult. To take from you the jewel you hold 168 so dear.

Mar. Prithee, tell me one thing first.

Boult. Come now, your one thing.

Mar. What canst thou wish thine enemy 172 to be?

Boult. Why, I could wish him to be my master, or rather, my mistress.

Mar. Neither of these are so bad as thou art, 176 Since they do better thee in their command.

157 malleable: *able to be moulded*
164 Marry, come up: *out upon you!*
165 with . . . bays: *with all the trimmings*
177 *Since they benefit thee in their employ*

Thou hold'st a place, for which the pained'st fiend
Of hell would not in reputation change;
Thou art the damned door-keeper to every   180
Coystril that comes inquiring for his Tib,
To the choleric fisting of every rogue
Thy ear is liable, thy food is such
As hath been belch'd on by infected lungs.   184

    Boult. What would you have me do? go to
the wars, would you? where a man may serve
seven years for the loss of a leg, and have not
money enough in the end to buy him a wooden 188
one?

Mar. Do anything but this thou doest. Empty
Old receptacles, or common sewers, of filth;
Serve by indenture to the common hangman: 192
Any of these ways are yet better than this;
For what thou professest, a baboon, could he speak,
Would own a name too dear. O that the gods
Would safely deliver me from this place!   196
Here, here's gold for thee.
If that thy master would gain by me,
Proclaim that I can sing, weave, sew, and dance,
With other virtues, which I'll keep from boast;   200
And I will undertake all these to teach.
I doubt not but this populous city will
Yield many scholars.

    Boult. But can you teach all this you speak of? 204

    Mar. Prove that I cannot, take me home again,
And prostitute me to the basest groom
That doth frequent your house.

    Boult. Well, I will see what I can do for thee; 208
if I can place thee, I will.

178 pained'st: *most tortured*   181 Coystril: *knave*
182 choleric fisting: *angry buffets*
195 Would . . . dear: *would think his race too good*

Mar. But, amongst honest women.

Boult. Faith, my acquaintance lies little a-
mongst them. But since my master and mistress 212
have bought you, there's no going but by their
consent; therefore I will make them acquainted
with your purpose, and I doubt not but I shall
find them tractable enough. Come; I'll do for 216
thee what I can; come your ways.   *Exeunt.*

ACT FIFTH

Enter Gower.

Marina thus the brothel 'scapes, and chances
Into an honest house, our story says.
She sings like one immortal, and she dances
As goddess-like to her admired lays;   4
Deep clerks she dumbs; and with her neeld composes
Nature's own shape, of bud, bird, branch, or berry,
That even her art sisters the natural roses;
Her inkle, silk, twin with the rubied cherry;   8
That pupils lacks she none of noble race,
Who pour their bounty on her; and her gain
She gives the cursed bawd. Here we her place,
And to her father turn our thoughts again,   12
Where we left him, on the sea. We there him lost,
Whence, driven before the winds, he is arriv'd
Here where his daughter dwells: and on this coast
Suppose him now at anchor. The city striv'd   16
God Neptune's annual feast to keep; from whence
Lysimachus our Tyrian ship espies,

5 Deep . . . dumbs: *she silences profound scholars*   neeld: *needle*
7 sisters: *is near akin to, very like*
8 inkle, silk: *linen or silk thread (used in embroidery)*
9 That: *so that*   16 striv'd: *outdid itself*

His banners sable, trimm'd with rich expense,
And to him in his barge with fervour hies.   20
In your supposing once more put your sight
Of heavy Pericles; think this his bark:
Where what is done in action—more, if might—
Shall be discover'd; please you, sit and hark.   *Exit.*

Scene One

[*On board Pericles' ship, off Mitylene. A pavilion on
deck, with a curtain before it; Pericles within
it, reclined on a couch*]

Enter Helicanus; to him two Sailors.

1. Sail. Where is Lord Helicanus? he can resolve
     you.
O! here he is.—
Sir, there's a barge put off from Mitylene,
And in it is Lysimachus, the governor,   4
Who craves to come aboard.   What is your will?
     Hel. That he have his.   Call up some gentlemen.
     2. Sail. Ho, gentlemen! my lord calls.

Enter two or three Gentlemen.

1. Gent. Doth your lordship call?   8
     Hel. Gentlemen, there is some of worth would come
     aboard;
I pray, greet him fairly.

Enter Lysimachus [with Attendants].

1. Sail. Sir,

21 supposing: *imagination*   22 heavy: *sad*
23 more, if might: *more would be shown if it were possible*
24 discover'd: *displayed*   Scene One; *cf. n.*
9 some of worth: *some important person*

This is the man that can, in aught you would,   12
Resolve you.

    Lys. Hail, reverend sir! The gods preserve you!

    Hel. And you, to outlive the age I am,
And die as I would do.

    Lys.   You wish me well.   16
Being on shore, honouring of Neptune's triumphs,
Seeing this goodly vessel ride before us,
I made to it to know of whence you are.

    Hel. First, what is your place?   20

    Lys. I am the governor of this place you lie before.

    Hel. Sir,
Our vessel is of Tyre, in it the king;
A man who for this three months hath not spoken   24
To anyone, nor taken sustenance
But to prorogue his grief.

    Lys. Upon what ground is his distemperature?

    Hel. 'Twould be too tedious to repeat;   28
But the main grief springs from the loss
Of a beloved daughter and a wife.

    Lys. May we not see him?

    Hel. You may;   32
But bootless is your sight: he will not speak
To any.

    Lys. Yet let me obtain my wish.

    Hel. Behold him. [*Pericles discovered.*] This was a
        goodly person,   36
Till the disaster that, one mortal night,
Drove him to this.

    Lys. Sir king, all hail! the gods preserve you! Hail,
        royal sir!   40

12 in aught you would: *about anything you want*
26 prorogue: *prolong*   27 distemperature: *disturbance of mind*
33 bootless . . . sight: *it will not profit you to see him*
37, 38 *Cf. n.*

Hel. It is in vain; he will not speak to you.

Lord. Sir,
We have a maid in Mitylene, I durst wager,
Would win some words of him.

Lys.   'Tis well bethought. 44
She questionless with her sweet harmony
And other chosen attractions, would allure,
And make a battery through his deafen'd parts
Which now are midway stopp'd: 48
She is all happy as the fair'st of all,
And with her fellow maids is now upon
The leafy shelter that abuts against
The island's side.   52

          [*Whispers Attendant, who goes out.*]

Hel. Sure, all's effectless; yet nothing we'll omit,
That bears recovery's name. But, since your kindness
We have stretch'd thus far, let us beseech you,
That for our gold we may provision have,   56
Wherein we are not destitute for want,
But weary for the staleness.

Lys.   O, sir, a courtesy,
Which if we should deny, the most just God
For every graff would send a caterpillar,   60
And so inflict our province.   Yet once more
Let me entreat to know at large the cause
Of your king's sorrow.

Hel.   Sit, sir, I will recount it to you;
But see, I am prevented.

[*Enter Attendant, with Marina, and a young Lady.*]

Lys.   O, here's   64

---

45 questionless: *undoubtedly*   47, 48 *Cf. n.*
51 abuts against: *borders on*   53 effectless: *useless*
54 That . . . name: *that promises recovery*
60 graff: *graft (of trees)*   61 inflict: *afflict*
62 at large: *fully*

The lady that I sent for.   Welcome, fair one!
Is 't not a goodly present?
    Hel.   She's a gallant lady.
    Lys. She's such a one, that were I well assur'd
Came of a gentle kind and noble stock,   68
I'd wish no better choice, and think me rarely wed.—
Fair one, all goodness that consists in bounty
Expect even here, where is a kingly patient:
If that thy prosperous and artificial feat   72
Can draw him but to answer thee in aught,
Thy sacred physic shall receive such pay
As thy desires can wish.
    Mar.   Sir, I will use
My utmost skill in his recovery,   76
Provided
That none but I and my companion maid
Be suffer'd to come near him.
    Lys.   Come, let us leave her;
And the gods make her prosperous!   80

The Song.

    Lys. Mark'd he your music?
    Mar.   No, nor look'd on us.
    Lys. See, she will speak to him.
    Mar. Hail, sir! my lord, lend ear.
    Per. Hum! ha! [*Pushes her away.*]   84
    Mar. I am a maid,
My lord, that ne'er before invited eyes,
But have been gaz'd on like a comet; she speaks,
My lord, that, may be, hath endur'd a grief   88
Might equal yours, if both were justly weigh'd.
Though wayward Fortune did malign my state,
My derivation was from ancestors

72 artificial feat: *feat of art*   80 S. d. The Song; *cf. n.*

Who stood equivalent with mighty kings;   92
But time hath rooted out my parentage,
And to the world and awkward casualties
Bound me in servitude.—[*Aside.*] I will desist;
But there is something glows upon my cheek,   96
And whispers in mine ear, 'Go not till he speak.'

   Per. My fortunes—parentage—good parentage—
To equal mine!—was it not thus? what say you?

   Mar. I said, my lord, if you did know my par-
       entage,   100
You would not do me violence.

   Per. I do think so. Pray you, turn your eyes upon
       me.
You 're like something that—. What country-woman?
Here of these shores?

   Mar.   No, nor of any shores;   104
Yet I was mortally brought forth, and am
No other than I appear.

   Per. I am great with woe, and shall deliver weeping.
My dearest wife was like this maid, and such a one 108
My daughter might have been: my queen's square
       brows;
Her stature to an inch; as wandlike-straight;
As silver-voic'd; her eyes as jewel-like,
And cas'd as richly; in pace another Juno;   112
Who starves the ears she feeds, and makes them
       hungry,
The more she gives them speech. Where do you live?

   Mar. Where I am but a stranger; from the deck
You may discern the place.

   Per.   Where were you bred? 116
And how achiev'd you these endowments, which

92 equivalent: *equally powerful*   94 awkward: *adverse*

You make more rich to owe?

    Mar. If I should tell my history, it would seem
Like lies, disdain'd in the reporting.   120

    Per. Prithee, speak;
Falseness cannot come from thee, for thou lookest
Modest as justice, and thou seem'st a palace
For the crown'd truth to dwell in. I will believe
    thee,   124
And make my senses credit thy relation
To points that seem impossible; for thou lookest
Like one I lov'd indeed. What were thy friends?
Didst thou not say when I did push thee back,— 128
Which was when I perceiv'd thee,—that thou cam'st
From good descending?

    Mar.   So indeed I did.

    Per. Report thy parentage. I think thou saidst
Thou hadst been toss'd from wrong to injury,   132
And that thou thought'st thy griefs might equal mine,
If both were open'd.

    Mar.   Some such thing
I said, and said no more but what my thoughts
Did warrant me was likely.

    Per.   Tell thy story;   136
If thine consider'd prove the thousandth part
Of my endurance, thou art a man, and I
Have suffer'd like a girl; yet thou dost look
Like Patience gazing on kings' graves, and smiling 140
Extremity out of act. What were thy friends?
How lost thou them? Thy name, my most kind virgin?
Recount, I do beseech thee. Come, sit by me.

    Mar. My name is Marina.

118 to owe: *by possessing*   125 relation: *tale*
126 To: *even as far as*   136 warrant: *assure*
137, 138 If . . . endurance; *cf. n.*
141 Extremity out of act: *so that extreme peril cannot strike*

Per.   Oh! I am mock'd,   144
And thou by some incensed god sent hither
To make the world to laugh at me.
     Mar.   Patience, good sir,
Or here I'll cease.
     Per.   Nay, I'll be patient.
Thou little know'st how thou dost startle me,   148
To call thyself Marina.
     Mar.   The name
Was given me by one that had some power,
My father, and a king.
     Per.   How! a king's daughter?
And call'd Marina?
     Mar.   You said you would believe me; 152
But, not to be a troubler of your peace,
I will end here.
     Per.   But are you flesh and blood?
Have you a working pulse? and are no fairy?
Motion!—Well; speak on.   Where were you born? 156
And wherefore call'd Marina?
     Mar.   Call'd Marina
For I was born at sea.
     Per.   At sea! what mother?
     Mar. My mother was the daughter of a king,
Who died the minute I was born,   160
As my good nurse Lychorida hath oft
Deliver'd weeping.
     Per.   O stop there a little.
This is the rarest dream that e'er dull sleep
Did mock sad fools withal.   This cannot be   164
My daughter, buried.—Well; where were you bred?
I'll hear you more, to the bottom of your story,
And never interrupt you.

162 Deliver'd: *told*

Mar. You scorn: believe me, 'twere best I did give
 o'er.   168
 Per. I will believe you by the syllable
Of what you shall deliver. Yet, give me leave:
How came you in these parts? where were you bred?
 Mar. The king my father did in Tarsus leave
 me,   172
Till cruel Cleon, with his wicked wife,
Did seek to murther me; and having woo'd
A villain to attempt it, who having drawn to do 't,
A crew of pirates came and rescu'd me;   176
Brought me to Mitylene. But, good sir,
Whither will you have me? Why do you weep? It
 may be
You think me an imposture; no, good faith;
I am the daughter to King Pericles,   180
If good King Pericles be.
 Per. Ho, Helicanus!
 Hel. Calls my lord?
 Per. Thou art a grave and noble counsellor, 184
Most wise in general; tell me, if thou canst,
What this maid is, or what is like to be,
That thus hath made me weep?
 Hel.   I know not; but
Here's the regent, sir, of Mitylene,   188
Speaks nobly of her.
 Lys.   She never would tell
Her parentage. Being demanded that,
She would sit still and weep.
 Per. O Helicanus! strike me, honour'd sir; 192
Give me a gash, put me to present pain,
Lest this great sea of joys rushing upon me

169 by the syllable: *every syllable*   174 woo'd: *solicited*
175 drawn: *i.e. his sword*

O'erbear the shores of my mortality,
And drown me with their sweetness.   Oh come
    hither,   196
Thou that begett'st him that did thee beget;
Thou that wast born at sea, buried at Tarsus,
And found at sea again.   O Helicanus!
Down on thy knees, thank the holy gods as loud   200
As thunder threatens us; this is Marina.
What was thy mother's name? tell me but that,
For truth can never be confirm'd enough,
Though doubts did ever sleep.

    Mar.   First, sir, I pray, 204
What is your title?

    Per. I am Pericles of Tyre: but tell me now
My drown'd queen's name, as in the rest you said
Thou hast been godlike perfect: 208
The heir of kingdoms, and another like
To Pericles thy father.

    Mar. Is it no more to be your daughter than
To say my mother's name was Thaisa?   212
Thaisa was my mother, who did end
The minute I began.

    Per. Now, blessing on thee! rise; th' art my child.
Give me fresh garments.   Mine own, Helicanus;   216
She is not dead at Tarsus, as she should have been,
By savage Cleon; she shall tell thee all;
When thou shalt kneel, and justify in knowledge
She is thy very princess.   Who is this?   220

    Hel. Sir, 'tis the governor of Mitylene,
Who, hearing of your melancholy state,
Did come to see you.

    Per.   I embrace you.

208 perfect: *correct*   211 Is it: *does it require*
215 th' art my child; *cf. n.*   217 should: *was reported to*
219 justify: *prove*

Give me my robes. I am wild in my beholding. 224
O heavens! bless my girl. But hark! what music?
Tell Helicanus, my Marina, tell him
O'er, point by point, for yet he seems to dote,
How sure you are my daughter. But, what music? 228

Hel. My lord, I hear none.

Per. None!

The music of the spheres! List, my Marina.

Lys. It is not good to cross him; give him way. 232

Per. Rarest sounds! Do ye not hear?

Lys. Music, my lord? I hear.

Per. Most heavenly music:
It nips me unto list'ning, and thick slumber
Hangs upon mine eyes; let me rest. [*Sleeps.*] 236

Lys. A pillow for his head!

So, leave him all. Well, my companion friends,
If this but answer to my just belief,
I'll well remember you. 240

Diana [appears to Pericles as in a vision].

Dia. My temple stands in Ephesus; hie thee thither,
And do upon mine altar sacrifice.
There, when my maiden priests are met together,
Before the people all, 244
Reveal how thou at sea didst lose thy wife;
To mourn thy crosses, with thy daughter's, call
And give them repetition to the life.
Or perform my bidding, or thou liv'st in woe; 248
Do it, and happy; by my silver bow!
Awake, and tell thy dream! [*Disappears.*]

Per. Celestial Dian, goddess argentine,

224 beholding: *appearance*
235 nips: *arrests*
240 S. d. Diana; *cf. n.*
247 to the life: *exact*
251 argentine: *silvery*

227 dote: *be bewildered*
238-240 Well . . . you; *cf. n.*
246 crosses: *trials*
248 Or: *either*

I will obey thee! Helicanus!
  Hel.   Sir?   252
  Per. My purpose was for Tarsus, there to strike
The inhospitable Cleon: but I am
For other service first: toward Ephesus
Turn our blown sails; eftsoons I'll tell thee why. 256
[*To Lysimachus.*] Shall we refresh us, sir, upon your
        shore,
And give you gold for such provision
As our intents will need?
  Lys. Sir,   260
With all my heart; and when you come ashore,
I have another suit.
  Per.   You shall prevail,
Were it to woo my daughter, for it seems
You have been noble towards her.
  Lys.   Sir, lend me your arm. 264
  Per. Come, my Marina.   *Exeunt.*

Scene Two

[*Enter Gower.*]

  Gower. Now our sands are almost run;
More a little, and then dumb.
This, my last boon, give me,
For such kindness must relieve me,   4
That you aptly will suppose
What pageantry, what feats, what shows,
What minstrelsy, and pretty din,
The regent made in Mitylen   8
To greet the king. So he thriv'd,
That he is promis'd to be wiv'd

---

256 eftsoons: *soon*   262 suit: *petition; cf. n*
5 aptly: *readily*

To fair Marina; but in no wise
Till he had done his sacrifice,   12
As Dian bade: whereto being bound,
The interim, pray you, all confound.
In feather'd briefness sails are fill'd,
And wishes fall out as they're will'd.   16
At Ephesus the temple see,
Our king and all his company.
That he can hither come so soon,
Is by your fancy's thankful doom.   [*Exit.*] 20

Scene Three

[*The Temple of Diana at Ephesus; Thaisa standing
near the altar, as high priestess; a number of Virgins on each side; Cerimon and other In-
habitants of Ephesus attending*]

[*Enter Pericles, with his Train; Lysimachus,
Helicanus, Marina, and a Lady.*]

Per. Hail, Dian! to perform thy just command,
I here confess myself the King of Tyre;
Who, frighted from my country, did wed
At Pentapolis the fair Thaisa.   4
At sea in childbed died she, but brought forth
A maid-child call'd Marina; who, O goddess!
Wears yet thy silver livery.   She at Tarsus
Was nurs'd with Cleon, whom at fourteen years   8
He sought to murder; but her better stars
Brought her to Mitylene, 'gainst whose shore
Riding, her fortunes brought the maid aboard us,

12 he: *Pericles*   14 confound: *consider gone*
15 In feather'd briefness: *swift as wings*
20 thankful doom: *decision for which I am thankful*
Scene Three The Temple of Diana at Ephesus; *cf. n.*
11 Riding: *modifies 'us.'*

Where, by her own most clear remembrance, she   12
Made known herself my daughter.

  Thai.   Voice and favour!
You are, you are—O royal Pericles!—   [*She faints.*]

  Per. What means the nun? she dies! help, gentle-
    men!

  Cer. Noble sir,   16
If you have told Diana's altar true,
This is your wife.

  Per.   Reverend appearer, no;
I threw her overboard with these very arms.

  Cer. Upon this coast, I warrant you.

  Per.   'Tis most certain. 20

  Cer. Look to the lady. O, she's but overjoy'd.
Early in blustering morn this lady was
Thrown upon this shore. I op'd the coffin,
Found there rich jewels; recovered her, and plac'd
    her   24
Here in Diana's temple.

  Per.   May we see them?

  Cer. Great sir, they shall be brought you to my
    house,
Whither I invite you. Look! Thaisa is
Recovered.

  Thai.   O! let me look!   28
If he be none of mine, my sanctity
Will to my sense bend no licentious ear,
But curb it, spite of seeing. O! my lord,
Are you not Pericles? Like him you spake,   32
Like him you are. Did you not name a tempest,
A birth, and death?

  Per.   The voice of dead Thaisa!

14 *Cf. n.*   **24** recovered: *revived*   **26** you: *for you*

Thai. That Thaisa am I, supposed dead
And drown'd.   36
  Per. Immortal Dian!
  Thai.   Now I know you better.
When we with tears parted Pentapolis,
The king my father gave you such a ring.
          [*Shows a ring.*]
  Per. This, this: no more, you gods! your present
   kindness   40
Makes my past miseries sports: you shall do well,
That on the touching of her lips I may
Melt and no more be seen. O! come, be buried
A second time within these arms.
  Mar.   My heart   44
Leaps to be gone into my mother's bosom.
       [*Kneels to Thaisa.*]
  Per. Look, who kneels here! Flesh of thy flesh,
   Thaisa;
Thy burden at the sea, and call'd Marina,
For she was yielded there.
  Thai.   Bless'd, and mine own! 48
  Hel. Hail, madam, and my queen!
  Thai.   I know you not.
  Per. You have heard me say, when I did fly from
   Tyre,
I left behind an ancient substitute.
Can you remember what I call'd the man?   52
I have nam'd him oft.
  Thai.   'Twas Helicanus then.
  Per. Still confirmation!
Embrace him, dear Thaisa; this is he.
Now do I long to hear how you were found,   56
How possibly preserv'd, and whom to thank,

38 parted: *left*   42 That: *if*

Besides the gods, for this great miracle.

Thai. Lord Cerimon, my lord; this man,
Through whom the gods have shown their power,
    that can   60
From first to last resolve you.

Per.   Reverend sir,
The gods can have no mortal officer
More like a god than you. Will you deliver
How this dead queen re-lives?

Cer.   I will, my lord,   64
Beseech you first, go with me to my house,
Where shall be shown you all was found with her;
How she came plac'd here in the temple;
No needful thing omitted.   68

Per. Pure Dian! bless thee for thy vision, and
Will offer night-oblations to thee. Thaisa,
This prince, the fair-betrothed of your daughter,
Shall marry her at Pentapolis. And now   72
This ornament
Makes me look dismal will I clip to form,
And what this fourteen years no razor touch'd,
To grace thy marriage-day I'll beautify.   76

Thai. Lord Cerimon hath letters of good credit, sir,
My father's dead.

Per. Heavens make a star of him! Yet there, my
    queen,
We'll celebrate their nuptials, and ourselves   80
Will in that kingdom spend our following days;
Our son and daughter shall in Tyrus reign.
Lord Cerimon, we do our longing stay
To hear the rest untold. Sir, lead 's the way.   84
                      [Exeunt.]

69 bless: *I bless*   73 *His hair and beard*
74 Makes: *which makes*

Gower.

In Antiochus and his daughter you have heard
Of monstrous lust the due and just reward:
In Pericles, his queen, and daughter, seen—
Although assail'd with fortune fierce and keen— 88
Virtue preserv'd from fell destruction's blast,
Led on by heaven, and crown'd with joy at last.
In Helicanus may you well descry
A figure of truth, of faith, of loyalty. 92
In reverend Cerimon there well appears
The worth that learned charity aye wears.
For wicked Cleon and his wife, when fame
Had spread their cursed deed, and honour'd name 96
Of Pericles, to rage the city turn,
That him and his they in his palace burn:
The gods for murder seemed so content
To punish; although not done, but meant. 100
So on your patience evermore attending,
New joy wait on you! Here our play has ending.

[*Exit.*]

FINIS.

NOTES

Dramatis Personæ. No list occurs in any of the Quartos. It appears first after the play in the Third Folio.

Act First. None of the Quartos have any division into acts and scenes. In the Folios the beginning is marked *Actus Primus Scena Prima.* Thereafter the acts, but not the scenes, are indicated. The division into scenes is the work of Malone.

I. Prologue. *Gower.* An English poet, ca. 1330-1408, whose *Confessio Amantis* contained the story of Pericles. See Appendix A, p. 112. Gower appears at the beginning of each act and at the end of the play, as well as before Act IV, Scene iv, and Act V, Scene ii. He speaks the prologue and the epilogue, and, in the character of Chorus, tells such parts of the tale as cannot be presented on the stage. There is another such prologue, epilogue, and chorus in *Henry V,* and in other Elizabethan plays outside of Shakespeare: e.g. Marlowe's *Doctor Faustus.* In Peele's (?) *Locrine* (ca. 1586) Ate introduces each act with dumb show, and supplies the epilogue. In three plays by Heywood, *The Golden Age, The Silver Age,* and *The Brazen Age,* Homer appears as Chorus. The device of a Chorus is apparently one of the features which the Elizabethan drama inherited from the Greek by way of Seneca. But the ancient chorus was present on the stage throughout the play, and its function was to supplement the action by moral observations, or ornament it by purely lyric passages; it was not used, as here, to supply information otherwise inaccessible to the audience.

I. Prologue. 6. *ember-eves.* The eves of ember days: days in each of the four seasons designated for fasting and prayer. The preceding evenings would be devoted to amusement.

holy-ales. The old editions read *Holydayes.* Richard Farmer is responsible for the present conjecture, on the analogy of *church-ales.* The word *holy-ales* is not known to occur elsewhere, but the editors have followed Farmer in a sentimental desire to preserve the semblance of rhyme, which is the one virtue of this prologue.

I. Prologue. 17, 18. *This Antioch, then, Antiochus the Great Built up, this city, for his chiefest seat.* Twine, at the beginning of the *Patterne of Painefull Adventures,* writes, 'The most famous and mightie king Antiochus . . . builded the goodly citie of Antiochia in Syria, and called it after his own name, as the chiefest seat of all his dominions.' (Quotations from Twine are according to the text in *Shakespeare's Library,* Part I, Vol. IV, edited by Hazlitt, London, 1875. Quotations from Gower are according to the edition by G. C. Macaulay, Oxford, 1901.) Antioch, on the river Orontes, was actually founded by Seleucus Nicator in 300 B.C., just after the battle of Ipsus, which assured him control of Asia Minor. It was enlarged by Antiochus Soter (280-261 B.C.), from whom it took its name. To Antiochus the Great (223-187 B.C.), here referred to, it owed only some further additions.

I. Prologue. 20. *I tell you what mine authors say.* This citation of authority is in imitation of Gower, e.g.

> 'the grete Antiochus
> Of whom that Antioche tok
> His ferst name, as seith the bok.'
>
> (*Confessio Amantis,* VIII. 274-276.)

'This yonge Prince, as seith the bok.'

(Ibid. 574.)

'And telle as the Croniques sein.'

(Ibid. 1546.)

I. Prologue. 22, 23. *Who died and left a female heir, So buxom, blithe, and full of face.* Cf. Milton, *L'Allegro,* 23, 24. 'Filled her with thee, a daughter fair, So buxom, blithe, and debonair.'

I. Prologue. 25, 26. *With whom the father liking took, And her to incest did provoke.* It may be that this slander on the memory of the great Antiochus originated in the fact that in 196-5 B.C. he married his son Antiochus to his daughter Laodice. This marrying of full brothers and sisters was common enough among the Persian kings, but this is the first instance of the practice among the Greek monarchs of Asia Minor, and it may well have created a scandal.

I. Prologue. 40. *As yon grim looks do testify.* In the *Confessio Amantis,* VIII. 363-365, the poet writes that, unless the suitor could guess the riddle,

'He scholde in certein lese his hed.
And thus there weren manye ded,
Here hevedes stondende [their heads standing] on
    the gate.'

Evidently Gower here points to the heads of the unlucky suitors, shown on the stage.

I. i. 1. *Young Prince of Tyre.* Tyre and Sidon were, from the earliest times, the chief seaports on the coast of Phœnicia. They were conquered by Alexander the Great, and thereafter were subject to one or other of the Greek dynasties that succeeded him. Tyre passed into the hands of Antiochus the Great for the first time in 221 B.C. For some years it was fought over by him and Ptolemy Philopatris, but, in 199-8 B.C. he got final control of it. It seems to have been governed by a satrap, whose subordinate power may be reflected in the title 'Prince,' which means, here, not the son of a reigning king, but a ruler under the king's authority. It is worth mentioning that in Godfrey of Viterbo's *Pantheon,* the hero is *rex Tyri et Sidonis.*

I. i. 10, 11. *The senate-house of planets all did
sit, To knit in her their best perfections.* The planets,
whose position was supposed to be of prime importance in determining human character and fortune,
conspired to make their influence all favorable. Cf.
Sidney's *Arcadia,* Book II (concerning the birth of
Pyrocles). 'The senate house of the planets was at
no time so set, for the decreeing of perfection in a
man.'

I. i. 13, 14. *Graces her subjects, and her thoughts
the king Of every virtue gives renown to men!* Her
mind is the sovereign served by the graces and all the
virtues that give renown to men.

I. i. 27. *Hesperides.* The daughters of Atlas,
celebrated in Greek mythology, from whose garden
Hercules brought back the golden apples which a
dragon had guarded. Here, the name is taken to be
that of the garden itself. Because of this line, 'Hesperides' appears in the first list of characters as the
name of the princess.

I. i. 59. *Of all say'd yet.* This is the Quarto reading. M. Mason conjectures 'In all save that,' meaning that she wishes him well, but does not want him
to read the riddle. Mitford conjectures 'Oh false!
and yet,' the exclamation addressed to herself because her wishing Pericles well is a betrayal of her
father's interest and her own. Steevens, approving
Mason's reading, remarks, with point, that one could
wish that the only speech the lady makes had been
intelligible.

I. i. 64-69. *The Riddle.* Gower's version of the
riddle is as follows:

> 'With felonie I am upbore,
> I ete and have it noght forbore
> My modres fleissh, whos housebonde
> My fader forto seche I fonde,
> Which is the Sone ek of my wif.'
>
> (*Confessio Amantis,* VIII. 405-9.)

The *Historia Apollonii Regis Tyrii* has 'Scelere vehor, maternam carnem vescor, quaero fratrem meum, meae matris filium, uxoris meae virum, nec invenio.' (I am carried away by sin, my mother's flesh I eat, I seek my brother, the son of my mother, the husband of my wife, and find him not.) It must be confessed that the riddle in its present state makes one think very lightly of the ingenuity of the gentlemen whose heads adorned the gate. The belief that young vipers eat their parents goes back to Herodotus III. 190. Cf. Blake, *Tiriel,*

'Serpents, not sons, wreathing around the bones of
    Tiriel!
Ye worms of death, feasting upon your aged
    parents' flesh.'

I. i. 96-100. *For vice repeated is like the wandering wind, Blows dust in others' eyes, to spread itself; And yet the end of all is bought thus dear, The breath is gone, and the sore eyes see clear To stop the air would hurt them.* As the wind spreads dust abroad, so the reporter of vice shocks the community. Yet when the wind has passed, people know from what quarter to protect themselves against more dust, and, though the informer may perish for it, people once warned of vice may be on their guard against it.

I. i. 103. *Kings are earth's gods.* As a matter of fact, Antiochus the Great, like all the house of Seleucus, did receive divine honors from his subjects.

I. i. 109. *Heaven, that I had thy head!* No one has yet explained why he did not have his head. If he had made no scruple to execute the previous suitors who had not guessed the riddle, it is astonishing that he hesitated a moment to silence Pericles, whose death was of the utmost importance to him. However, the playwright is not to blame; both Gower and the *Gesta Romanorum* have this curious delay of the sentence.

I. i. 112-115. *Your exposition misinterpreting, We might proceed to cancel off your days; Yet hope, succeeding from so fair a tree As your fair self, doth tune us otherwise.* Since your explanation misinterprets, we might proceed to put you to death, but, judging by your fair appearance, we hope for better things from you, and are inclined to do otherwise.

I. ii. S. d. *Enter Pericles with his Lords.* This is the reading of the Quarto. Either the Lords must be supposed to go out again at the words *Let none disturb us,* or Pericles soliloquizes in their presence. After line 33, the direction *Enter all the Lords to Pericles* is not easily explained if 'his Lords' are supposed to be already on the stage, yet to have them appear and disappear at his first words would be a dramatic absurdity. It is certainly more convenient to follow the directions of Craig, who makes Pericles enter alone, and speak his first words *to those without.*

I. iii. 4. *he was a wise fellow.* This is a reference to Barnabe Riche's *Soldier's Wishe to Britons Welfare, or Captain Skill and Captain Pill,* of 1604: 'I will therefore commende the poet Philipides, who being dimaunded by King Lisimachus, what favour he might doe unto him for that he loved him, made this answere to the King, "that your majestie would never impart unto me any of your secrets." '

I. iii. 34. *But since my landing I have understood.* Since is used in a double sense, both temporal and causative. But because after I landed I found out.

I. iv. *Tarsus.* Tarsus in Cilicia lies about ten miles from the sea of Cyprus, and less than a hundred, in a straight line, from Antioch, though perhaps twice that distance by road. It was a part of Antiochus' empire, and would therefore be no safe refuge for an enemy of his. It is not likely that, at this time, it was under a special satrap, such as the governor here depicted, but it was then, as later, 'no mean city.'

I. iv. 8, 9. *Here they're but felt, and seen with mischief's eyes, But like to groves, being topped they higher rise.* If the reading is right, it must mean that, at present, the woes of Tarsus are evident only to the sufferers themselves in the light of their own misfortune, but a comparison with other calamities would make them at once better known and harder to bear. For *mischief's* Steevens would read *mistful;* Singer, *mistie;* Walker, *misery's;* Kennear, *weakness.* But *mischief* commonly means 'calamity.' *Topped* means 'trimmed at the top,' which makes the trees grow higher.

I. iv. 93. *the Troyan horse.* The huge hollow horse, filled with Greek warriors, which the Trojans unsuspiciously dragged into the town, and which brought about the fall of Troy. The *bloody veins* are, of course, the soldiers inside, intent on shedding blood. The tale of the Trojan horse is given in Gower, *Confessio Amantis,* I. 1060-1189.

I. iv. 95. *Are stor'd with corn to make your needy bread.* To make bread for your needy citizens. T. S. Graves, in an article entitled *On the Date and Significance of Pericles,* in *Modern Philology* for January, 1916, points out that a Venetian ambassador in England is said to have gone 'to a play called *Pericles* which cost (him) more than 20 crowns.' Among other circumstances bearing on the date, is the fact that late in the year 1606, and early in 1607, the ambassador was attempting to get grain shipped to Venice, to relieve the famine there. It is Mr. Graves' opinion that the performance of *Pericles* in question was produced at this time at the expense of the Venetian ambassador, who hoped that the tale of Pericles relieving the distressed citizens would arouse sympathy for his own mission. The arguments of the article are sometimes rather tenuous, but it does furnish an interesting suggestion as to the date of the first performance.

II. i. S. d. *Pentapolis.* Here understood to be one city, but, in fact, the 'Five Cities' of Cyrene, Apollonia, Berenice, Barca and Asinoë, whose territory comprised the northern part of the district known as Cyrenaica, on the north coast of Africa, to the west of Egypt. In the time of Antiochus, it was a possession of Ptolemy, and had no resident monarch.

II. i. S. d. *Enter three Fishermen.* The older versions of the story have one fisherman only. The change acquires an added interest from a comparison with the fishermen who appear at the beginning of the Second Act of the *Rudens* of the Latin dramatist, Plautus. In that case also the scene is on the coast of Cyrenaica, immediately after a great storm in which some of the characters have been shipwrecked. It is another fisherman who draws up out of the sea the wallet containing proof of the heroine's identity, an incident slightly like the netting of the armor in II. i. 129. These resemblances may, of course, be accidental, but one is tempted to think that Shakespeare, who was familiar with Plautus (cf. *The Comedy of Errors,* founded on the *Menæchmi,* and *Hamlet* II. ii. 428, 429: *Seneca cannot be too heavy, nor Plautus too light*) may have revised this scene, thinking of the similar situation in the *Rudens.* K. Deighton, in the introduction to *Pericles* in the *Arden Shakespeare,* concludes, from considerations of style, that Shakespeare rewrote the scene.

II. i. 12. *Pilch.* The name of an outer garment of skin or leather.

II. i. 58-60. This passage certainly means nothing as it stands, and requires somewhat violent emendation before it can mean anything. Steevens conjectures the loss of the last line of Pericles' preceding speech, which he restores as follows:

'The day is rough and thwarts your occupations,' and then reads:

Second Fish. Honest! good fellow, what's that? If it be not a day fits you, scratch it out of the calendar, and nobody will look after it.

This has the merit of sense, if not of probability.

II. i. 65. *tennis-court.* The game is, of course, not lawn-tennis, but court-tennis, and Pericles thinks of himself as enclosed on all sides by wind and water. Whatever was the nature of the Greek game of ball, it must be admitted that the phrase is an anachronism in the mouth of a hero of the second century B.C. In Twine's novel, tennis was the game which the king of Pentapolis was playing when Apollonius encountered him. Cf. Sidney's *Arcadia,* Book V, 'In such a shadow . . . mankind lives . . . that . . . they . . . are like tenis bals tossed by the racket of the higher powers.'

II. i. 120. *joust and tourney.* The episode is transplanted. The joust is, of course, an anachronism. Both Gower and Twine have the tourneying and dancing in connection with the celebration of Pericles' marriage to Thaisa. Cf. *Confessio Amantis,* VIII. 965. 'Thei jouste first and after daunce.' And *Patterne of Painefull Adventures,* Chap. VII, 'I may not discourse at large of the liberall challenges made and proclaimed at the tilt, barriers, running at the ring, ioco di can, managing fierce horses, running a foote, and daunsing in armour.' It may have been developed, in the play, in deference to the court of James, which affected mediæval chivalry. The discovery of the armor is an innovation of our author.

II. i. 124, 125. 'Perhaps the meaning may be this: "What a man cannot accomplish he may lawfully endeavor to obtain"; as, for instance, his wife's affections.' (M. Mason.)

II. i. 137. *brace.* Properly armor for the arms. Here apparently extended to mean the whole suit.

II. i. 147. *target.* Properly a light shield. Here the whole suit of armor.

II. ii. 14, 15. *'Tis now your honour, daughter, to explain The labour of each knight in his device.* In the novel, the shields are presented to the princess by the knights' pages, and she passes them to her father, who explains the mottos to her.

II. ii. 27. *Piu,* which is Italian, is an error for the Spanish word *Mas.*

II. ii. 37. *touchstone.* A flint-like stone on which gold was rubbed and its purity ascertained by the color of the metal rubbed off.

II. ii. 57. There is an obvious inversion here. Either we should punctuate, *The outward habit by, the inward man,* or transpose *outward* and *inward.*

II. iii. 17. *And you're her labour'd scholar.* The word *scholar* suggests that the labor was his, yet the preceding lines imply that art makes the artist, so that *labour'd scholar* should mean 'carefully wrought creation.'

II. iii. 23. *Sir, yonder is your place.* Cf. Gower, *Confessio Amantis,* VIII. 711-716:

> 'At Soupertime natheles
> The king amiddes al the pres
> Let clepe [called] him up among hem alle,
> And bad his Mareschall of halle
> To setten him in such degre
> That he upon him myhte se.'

II. iii. 29. *These cates resist me, she but thought upon.* Cf. Wilkins' novel: 'Both king and daughter at one instant were so strucke in love with the noblenesse of his woorth that they could not spare so much

time to satisfie themselves with the delicacie of their
viands for talking of his prayses.'

II. iii. 62, 63. *And princes not doing so are like
to gnats, Which make a sound, but kill'd are wonder'd
at.* When the gnat is killed, one wonders that so
small a creature could make so much sound. So it is
a matter of wonder that an unworthy prince can
make such a stir.

II. iii. 81-85. The novel almost exactly reproduces
this passage. 'Pericles . . . thus returneth what hee is,
that hee was a gentleman of Tyrc, his name Pericles,
his education beene in Artes and Armes who looking
for adventures in the world was by the rough and
unconstant Seas most unfortunately bereft both of
shippes and men, and after shipwrecke thrown upon
that shoare.' This is the first we hear of his looking
for adventure; when he left Tyre he was seeking only
safety.

II. iii. 106, 107. *Oh! that's as much as you would
be denied Of your fair courtesy.* That is as much as
to say that you desire not to receive the compliment
you deserve.

II. iv. 9, 10. *A fire from heaven came and shrivell'd
up Their bodies.* Neither Antiochus the Great, nor
any other Antiochus of whom history speaks, died in
such a manner. Antiochus the Great made his son,
Seleucus Philopator, joint king, in 188 B.C., and set
out on an expedition to the east from which he never
returned.

II. iv. 31-33. *And be resolv'd he lives to govern
us, Or dead, give's cause to mourn his funeral, And
leave us to our free election.* This is the reading of
the Quarto, and is perfectly intelligible without
emendation, though the construction is somewhat
loose. It means: And we shall be assured that he
lives to govern us, or, if he be dead, do you give

us opportunity to mourn his funeral and then allow us to elect his successor.

II. v. 3, 4. *for this twelvemonth she'll not undertake A married life.* This little fiction is described by Clarke as 'quite characteristic of the waggish tendency to stratagem shown by the royal old gentleman.'

II. v. 10, 11. *Diana's livery . . . the eye of Cynthia.* Diana is the virgin goddess and also the goddess of the moon, here addressed as Cynthia.

II. v. 28. Gower, after his description of the feast of III. iii., has Apollonius exhibit his skill in music (*Confessio Amantis,* VIII. 777-782):

> 'He takth the Harpe and in his wise [skill]
> He tempreth [tuneth] and of such assise
> Singende he harpeth forth withal,
> That as a vois celestial
> Hem thoghte it souneth in here ere,
> As thogh that he an Angel were.'

Variants are given in Wilkins' novel, and in Twine. Some such scene must have been in the playwright's mind, though the play gives no hint of it. Sykes argues from this that the play is founded on the novel (cf. Appendix C, p. 121), but it is quite as possible that the playwright was following Gower or Twine as that he was following the Wilkins novel. In any case he thought of the incident as part of the plot, and it may have been written into the play and later rejected.

II. v. 93. 'I cannot dismiss the foregoing scene, till I have expressed the most supreme contempt of it. Such another gross, nonsensical dialogue would be sought for in vain among the earliest and rudest efforts of the British theatre. It is impossible not to wish that the *Knights* had horsewhipped *Simonides* and that *Pericles* had kicked him off the stage.' (Steevens.)

III. Gower 15-19. *By many a dern and painful perch, Of Pericles the careful search By the four opposing coigns, Which the world together joins, Is made with all due diligence.* The careful search for Pericles is made with all due diligence through the four corners of the world by many a wild and painful journey. A *perch* is literally a measure of land, five yards and a half in length.

III. Gower 55-57. *action may Conveniently the rest convey, Which might not what by me is told.* Action, which could not well convey what I have told, may conveniently convey the rest.

III. i. The critics are generally agreed that Shakespeare's hand first appears in this scene, and that it is mostly, if not entirely, his. Cf. the storm in *King Lear* III. ii., and at the beginning of *The Tempest*. He may, however, have retouched passages previous to this.

III. i. 1. *rebuke these surges.* Cf. Matt. 9. 26, 'Then he arose and rebuked the winds and the sea, and there was a great calm.'

III. i. 24-26. *We here below, Recall not what we give, and therein may Vie honour with you.* We mortals do not take back what we give, and, in this respect, may contend for honor with the gods.

III. i. 47. *Sir, your queen must overboard.* Many interesting instances of this common superstition have been discovered, the earliest, apparently, being a passage in Plutarch, who describes how Cato's ship was storm-tossed on his return from Thrace because he refused the pleas of his friends to put the ashes of his brother in another vessel.

III. ii. *Ephesus.* A town in Lydia on the east coast of the Mediterranean. The fact that it is some six hundred miles from Tyre, and three hundred to the north, is sufficient evidence of the violence of the storm. It was a part of the empire of Antiochus.

III. ii. 35. *my aid.* A reference to the pupil, Machaon, whom Twine makes responsible for Thaisa's recovery.

III. ii. 97. *sets.* Shakespeare frequently employs the old northern English plural ending in -s.

III. ii. 103. *twice rich.* 'Because it is blessed with the sight not only of the cases with golden fringes, but of the jewels that they contain.' (Sykes.) Cf. *Arcadia,* Book III, 'Her fair lids then hiding her fairer eyes, seemed unto him sweet boxes of mother of pearl, rich in themselves but containing in them far richer jewels.'

III. ii. 105, 106. *O dear Diana! Where am I? Where's my lord? What world is this?* The recovery of Thaisa is closely copied from Gower, *Confessio Amantis,* VIII. 1192-1207:

'Thei leide hire on a couche softe,
And with a scheete warmed ofte
Hire colde brest began to hete,
Hire herte also to flacke and bete.
This Maister hath hire every joignt
With certein oile and balsme enoignt,
And putte a liquour in hire mouth
Which is to fewe clerkes couth, [known]
So that sche coevereth ate laste:
And ferst hire yhen up sche caste,
And whan sche more of strengthe cawhte,
Hire armes bothe forth sche strawhte,
Hield up hire hond and pitously
Sche spak and seide, "Ha, wher am I?
Where is my lord, what world is this?" '

III. iii. 6, 7. The reading of the First Quarto is: *Your shakes of fortune, though they hant you mortally Yet glance full wonderingly on us.* The Second changes *hant* to *haunt.* This must mean: Your changes of fortune, following you with a fatal persistence, affect us remarkably, also. But this use of

wonderingly is strange, and it seems better to follow
Steevens in reading *wanderingly* in the sense of
wandering from the mark. Steevens would also read
shafts for *shakes,* and *hurt* for *hant,* making a con-
sistent figure.

III. iv. 9. We must suppose that the good queen's
memory, which had been so shaken that she could not
recall the birth of her daughter, had also lost the
recollection of her husband's rank and destination.
Otherwise, it is hard to see why she did not follow
him to Tyre.

III. iv. 10. *vestal livery.* Properly the garb of
the virgins who served in the temple of Vesta, goddess
of the hearth. Here merely the garb of a priestess
of the virgin goddess, Diana.

IV. Gower 32. *the dove of Paphos.* Paphos, a
town in Cyprus, was a seat of the worship of Venus,
who was said to have risen from the waves there.
Doves were sacred to her as the goddess of beauty.

IV. Gower 34, 35. *All praises which are paid as
debts And not as given.* All praise her as though they
owe the praise, not as though they were bestowing it.

IV. Gower 47-50. *Only I carried winged time
Post on the lame feet of my rime Which never could
I so convey Unless your thoughts went on my way.*
I only conveyed briefly in my verse the idea of the
time elapsed, which you would not have understood
without my guidance.

IV. i. 96. *Valdes.* Malone remarked that the
name may probably have been taken from Don Pedro
de Valdes, who was an admiral in the Spanish Ar-
mada, and, being captured by Drake in 1588, was
imprisoned at Dartmouth.

IV. ii. *Mitylene.* The chief town of Lesbos,
in the Ægean Sea. It revolted from Antiochus and
joined the Romans, who had just begun to concern
themselves with Asiatic politics.

IV. ii. 37. *hatched.* Closed with a hatch or half
door with an open space above, taken as a characteristic of brothels by former editors. But, surely,
the context demands a reputable dwelling house.

IV. ii. 43 S. d. *Enter Boult, with the Pirates and
Marina.* Seneca Rhetor (*Floruit* 15 A.D.) in one of
his illustrative law cases (*Controversiæ* I. 2) gives
proof either that this part of the story has an ancient
source, or that the situation was not unique, by in-
troducing a virgin, captured by pirates and sold to a
procurer.

IV. iii. It is interesting to note the difference between this version and that of Twine in the *Patterne
of Painefull Adventures,* Chapter XII. 'But Stranguilio himselfe consented not to this treason, but so
soone as hee heard of the foule mischaunce, beeing as
it were a mopte [bewildered], and mated with heaui-
nesse and griefe, he clad himselfe in mourning aray,
and lamented that wofull case, saying, Alas, in what
a mischiefe am I wrapped? what might I doe, or say
herein?—Then casting his eies vp towards heauen,
O God said hee, thou knowest that I am innocent
¿rom the bloud of silly [innocent] Tharsia, which
thou hast to require at Dionisiades handes: and there-
withall he looked towards his wife, saying: Thou
wicked woman, tell me, how hast thou made away
prince Apollonius daughter? thou that liuest both to
the slaunder of God, and man? Dionisiades answered
in manie wordes euermore excusing herselfe, and,
moderating the wrath of Stranguilio, shee counter-
feited a fained sorrowe by attiring her selfe and her
daughter in mourning apparell.' It will be seen that
Cleon and Dionyza differ from Stranguilio and
Dionysiades in proportion as they resemble Macbeth
and Lady Macbeth. There is something of Lady
Macbeth in Dionyza in the scene with Leonine, too.
We have excellent evidence, then, for concluding that

this is a scene which Shakespeare rewrote from a less elaborate and less dramatic original.

IV. iii. 46. *harpy.* A mythical, malignant fowl with a human face. Dionyza's face deceives the victims whom she destroys with her talons.

IV. iii. 49, 50. *You are like one that superstitiously Do swear to the gods that winter kills the flies.* In fear of the gods you swear that the killing was not of your doing and was beyond your control.

V. i. In the performance of 1854 in which Phelps took the part of Pericles, this recognition scene is the only one which called forth the enthusiasm of John Oxenham, who wrote, in the *Times,* 'This scene was the only opportunity for acting throughout the piece, and Mr. Phelps availed himself of it most felicitously.'

V. i. 37, 38. *Till the disaster that, one mortal night, Drove him to this.* Surely, this is meant to refer to the night when his wife died and his daughter was born. But it was not that night, but the discovery of his daughter's supposed death that 'drove him to this.' The Quartos read *wight* for *night.*

V. i. 47, 48. *And make a battery through his deafen'd parts Which now are midway stopp'd.* And force an entrance to his mind through his ears which are now shut.

V. i. 80 S. d. *The Song.* Gower merely records the fact that she sang 'lich an angele,' but Twine gives the following song:

'Among the harlots foule I walke,
    yet harlot none am I:
The Rose amongst the Thorns grows,
    and is not hurt thereby.
The thiefe that stole me, sure I thinke,
    is slaine before this time,

> A bawd me bought, yet am I not
>   defilde by fleshly crime.
> Were nothing pleasanter to me,
>   than parents mine to know:
> I am the issue of a king,
>   my bloud from kings doth flow.
> I hope that God will mend my state,
>   and send a better day.
> Leaue off your teares, plucke vp your heart,
>   and banish care away.
> Shew gladnesse in your countenance,
>   cast vp your cheerfull eyes:
> That God remaines that once of nought
>   created earth and skies.
> He will not let in care and thought
>   you still to liue, and all for nought.'

It is impossible to tell how much like this was the song in the play, but it is attractive to think of an incidental lyric by Shakespeare, like Ariel's songs in *The Tempest,* on the theme 'The rose amongst the thorns grows and is not hurt thereby.' During the song, the others withdraw a little.

V. i. 137, 138. *If thine consider'd prove the thousandth part Of my endurance.* If what thou hast endured prove, on consideration, the thousandth part of what I have.

V. i. 215. *th' art my child.* The rediscovery of lost children is a very common feature of the romantic dramas of the Greek New Comedy.

V. i. 238-240. Malone suggests that these lines should be given to Marina, and that *companion friend* should be read, referring to the *companion maid* of line 78. But it is possible that the whole speech belongs to Helicanus.

V. i. 240 S. d. *Diana.* This appearance of a god in a dream is characteristic, not of ancient drama, but of ancient romance. In Heliodorus, *Æthiopica,*

III. ii., Apollo and Diana appear to the hero, Cala-siris, in a vision and tell him to return to his own country. In Longus, *Daphnis and Chloe,* IV. 34, Dionysophanes dreams that the Nymphs tell him to exhibit the tokens of Chloe before the people of Mitylene, which leads to the discovery of her identity.

V. i. 262. *I have another suit.* As Pericles sur-mises, he is about to ask for Marina's hand. In Twine's version, as soon as the governor finds that she is of royal parentage, 'using the benefite of the time,' he kneels to Apollonius without more ado, and rises his prospective son-in-law. In Gower, the idea does not seem to have occurred to him until the cele-brations attending Apollonius' entry into Mitylene.

V. iii. S. d. *The Temple of Diana at Ephesus.* The first shrine on this location goes back to the eighth century B.C. The fifth and last temple, the one here referred to, was built in the latter half of the fourth century B.C. and stood until the third century A.D. For its importance, cf. Acts 19. 27. It would make a fine scene for the climax of a pagan romance.

V. iii. 14. *You are, you are—O royal Pericles!* Compare the very similar ending of *The Comedy of Errors,* where the Abbess rediscovers the husband from whom she has been parted at sea.

APPENDIX A

Sources of the Play

The ultimate source of the story is undoubtedly a pagan Greek romance, probably by a writer of Asia Minor or Egypt, certainly later than the second century B.C., and certainly earlier than the sixth century A.D. It apparently falls somewhere in the first three centuries of the Christian era. The story is laid in the time of Antiochus the Great (second century B.C.), and, though it is full of historical inaccuracies, as will be seen from the notes, it preserves enough reminiscence of the actual conditions to make it almost certain that it came from an age before the break-up of the Roman empire had obliterated all memory of the preceding Greek empire in Asia. The Greek original, of a type familiar from other works, is lost, but it is represented by a great number of Latin manuscripts, bearing the general title *Historia Apollonii regis Tyrii*, which are more or less close translations with a certain amount of later Christian coloring. These vary considerably in content and in age, the earliest being of the ninth century, but the main outline of the story is constant, and is that reproduced in *Pericles, Prince of Tyre*. The original Latin version probably dates from the fifth century A.D. At least two editions were printed before 1500. In the twelfth century, Godfrey of Viterbo used the story in his *Pantheon*, a verse chronicle of events, beginning with Adam. It was partly from this work that Gower borrowed the tale. It was also included, in the thirteenth or fourteenth century, by the anonymous compiler of the *Gesta Romanorum*, which is the basis of Twine's version. From one or other of the Latin manuscripts, from the *Pantheon*, and from the *Gesta Romanorum*, a multitude of variants arose, in a dozen different languages.

John Gower, an English poet, contemporary with Chaucer, wrote, about 1390, the *Confessio Amantis* (first printed, by Caxton, in 1483), a collection of tales illustrating the seven deadly sins. In the Eighth Book, which deals with lechery, occurs the case of Antiochus and his daughter, which serves as an introduction to the whole story of Apollonius. It is written in rhymed tetrameter, like most of the Gower choruses in the play. In lines 271-273 he states his obligation to Godfrey of Viterbo:

'Of a Cronique in daies gon,
The which is cleped [named] Pantheon,
In loves cause I rede thus'—

But he is also influenced by the Latin narrative. There are several instances of his agreement with the *Historia Apollonii regis Tyrii* where he differs from Godfrey, besides certain changes for which he is himself responsible. Gower is one of the immediate sources of the play; the other is 'The Patterne of Painefull Aduentures, Containing the most excellent, pleasant, and variable Historie of the strange accidents that befell vnto Prince Apollonius, the Lady Lucina his wife and Tharsia his daughter. Wherein the vncertaintie of this world, and the fickle state of mans life are liuely described. Gathered into English by Laurence Twine Gentleman. Imprinted at London by William How. 1576.'[1] This is a translation of the *Gesta Romanorum* version. Twine was an Oxford graduate of some repute as a poet, but, except for the song (cf. n. on V. i. 80) and three rhymed

---

[1] The title is so given by Sidney Lee (Oxford facsimile of *Pericles*, p. 8), apparently on the assumption that it was identical with the later editions except for the imprimatur. The title given in the Stationers' Registers is 'The most excellent variable and pleasant history of the strange adventures of Prince Apollonius, Lucina his wife, and Tharsa his daughter.'

riddles in this work, his poetry has disappeared. No copies of the original edition are known to exist, but it was reprinted, once without date, and again in 1607.

As Gower had professed to follow Godfrey, so the play opens with an acknowledgment of Gower as its literary father. This announcement is made through the introduction of the poet himself, talking a villainous counterfeit Middle English, as Chorus. Like Gower, the playwright uses a second source as well, but, in this case, Twine's novel furnished only a few passages. The interview between Cleon and Dionyza, for example (IV. iii., cf. n.), is modelled on the novel, and not on the poem. Here and there incidents and phrases show Twine's influence, but Gower must be acknowledged to be the chief source. When the two differ as to the names of characters, the play (except in the case of Cerimon) prefers the form given by Gower. But there is some originality in the matter of names. Stranguilio, Arthestrathes, and Athenagoras become Cleon, Simonides, and Lysimachus respectively—*metri causa,* one would suppose. Leonine, the keeper of the brothel in Gower (his name doubtless reminiscent of the Latin *leno*) becomes Dionyza's servant, whose earlier name was Theophilus. Boult is invented by the playwright. Gower leaves the hero's wife nameless and calls the daughter Thaise; Thaisa[1] now becomes the mother, while the daughter is named Marina,[2] from her birth at sea. Most important of all, the prince himself, hitherto consistently known as Apollonius, becomes Pericles. It is possible that there may be some recollection of the great Athenian statesman, though there is little enough similarity, but it seems more likely that the name was suggested by Pyrocles, the hero of the romance, *The*

[1] In Act III, Scene iv, the Quartos read *Tharsa;* Twine's name for the daughter was Tharsia.

[2] But the Quartos of 1609 and 1611 have *MARIANA* on the title-page.

Countesse of Pembroke's Arcadia written by Philippe Sidnei, published in 1590. There are other instances of similarity (e.g. I. i. 10, 11, cf. n.) which make it probable that Sidney's book was fresh in the playwright's mind.

The consideration of George Wilkins' novel is reserved for Appendix C.

APPENDIX B

The History of the Play

The literary history of the play begins with the following entry in the Stationers' Registers, in the year 1608:

20 Maij

Entered [to Edward Blount] for his copie under thandes of Sir George Buck knight and Master Warden Seton A booke called. *The booke of Pericles prynce of Tyre* vjd.

But Blount did not publish the play, for what reason cannot be determined. It was published in 1609 by Henry Gosson, in two quarto editions. The title-pages of these are identical, but numerous small differences in the text make it clear that one is a reprint of the other. The question of precedence is discussed, by P. Z. Round, in the introductions to the Quarto Facsimiles printed by Pretorius in 1886. He decides, as do the Cambridge editors, in favor of the British Museum copy C. 12h. 5. (distinguished by the first stage direction *Enter Gower,* while the other has *Eneer Gower*) as the First Quarto, and that decision is adopted in the present edition.[1] The Quartos of

---

[1] It should be noted that the facsimile of the First Quarto in the Bodleian Library, published, in 1905, by Sidney Lee, differs from the British Museum copy. The Oxford facsimile has the following divergent readings:

II Gower 24 *And hid in Tent to murdered him* (Q1 *And had intent to murder him;* Q2 *And hid intent to murder him*). (This is noted by the Cambridge editors.)

II. i. 126 *pary* (Q1 & 2 *pray*)

II. i. 127 *yeat* (Q1 & 2 *yet*)

II. i. 152 *di'e* (Q1 *do'e;* Q2 *di'e*)

V. i. 34 *sight, hee will* (Q1 *sight see, will;* Q2 *sight, hee will*)

These differences are not important, but the coincidences

1609 were followed by another in 1611, a fourth in 1619, a fifth in 1630, which exhibits two varieties of title-page, and a sixth in 1635. Although excluded from the First Folio, of 1623, and the Second Folio, of 1632, it was included in the second impression of the Third Folio, of 1664, and in the Fourth Folio, of 1685. The first critical edition was that of Nicolas Rowe, in 1709, republished in 1714. Pope rejected the play as spurious, and the next editor of a collective edition to publish it was Malone, in 1780. In 1734, however, two separate 12mo editions appeared, one by R. Walker, the other by J. Tonson. All editors since, except J. Keightley, in 1864, have printed it. The text of the first Quartos is very corrupt. Not only are misprints common, but occasionally passages of prose are printed in lines like verse, and very often blank verse is run together like prose, or divided without the slightest attention to meter. It seems likely that the source of the text was a shorthand copy, made at a performance. This would explain not only the confusion of prose and verse, but certain verbal errors as well (e.g. *Pompey* for *pompae* II. ii. 30). Whatever the source, it is sufficiently apparent that no qualified person reviewed the text before its first printing. Nor did it have the benefit of comparison with a correct copy thereafter, for the subsequent history of the text is a course of careless mistakes, varied with unintelligent corrections, until the last state thereof is worse than the first. Occasionally, but very rarely, a true reading is found in one of the later editions. Rowe began the laudable attempt to make the play intelligible. In this he was followed by Steevens and Malone, who attacked the multitudinous problems with a praise-

with the Second Quarto suggest that a full collation of the seven other known copies of the First Quarto would be desirable.

worthy courage and industry. Very little was over-
looked, and every edition since their time has borne
the marks of their learned labors. But it was the
style of their time for editors to allow themselves
licenses in regard to emendation which stricter critical standards would not approve. At times they re-
store rather what the dramatist ought to have written
than what he did write. The state of the text, and
the character of the non-Shakespearean parts of the
play lend themselves only too readily to emendations
of that sort, so that many passages in the Steevens-
Malone editions are pretty certainly not what the
author wrote, though they are unquestionably much
smoother reading. This would do no harm, if it had
not proved so much easier to adopt their results than
to form a new text out of the original chaos, that
many an unsound conjecture has received the sanction
of continued repetition, and become an established
part of the play. The result has been assisted by the
fact that the critics do not always look for authority
before they argue, and more than one ingenious deduc-
tion has been made from a conjecture mistaken for a
fact. A scholarly, detailed reëxamination of the
early copies will ultimately yield a better text than
is now available.

The first edition presupposes that the play had already been acted. It is generally conceded that it had
been acted before the entry in the Stationers' Registers in 1608. Evidence that it was produced as
early as 1606 is presented by T. S. Graves (cf. n. on
I. iv. 95). The first reference to it was in 1609, in an
anonymous rhyme. Several other seventeenth century
notices of it strayed into print, but the only two that
are worth repeating are the reference of Ben Jonson
in 'Come leave the loathed stage' to 'some mouldy tale
like Pericles,' and the couplet from Dryden's prologue
to Davenant's *Circe:*

> '*Shakespeare's* own Muse her *Pericles* first bore,
> The Prince of *Tyre* was elder than the *Moore*.'

Dryden, then, explained the defects of the piece on the ground of Shakespeare's inexperience. In this he was wrong. Jonson merely testifies that the play had more success than it deserved, which would, indeed, be evident enough from the profusion of quarto editions. We hear of its production on May 24, 1619, at the Court, in honor of the French ambassador, and, on June 10, 1631, at the Globe Theatre 'upon the cessation of the plague.' There is no doubt that there were many successful performances of which there is no record. According to Downes,[1] Betterton was 'highly applauded' for his acting in the title rôle, probably in 1659. During the Restoration period, it fell into oblivion, whence it has seldom emerged. In 1738, George Lillo recast the drama, starting with the present Act IV, but making a three-act play of it. The change benefits the play somewhat, in the points of unity and decency, but the new matter is weak. This composite piece, named *Marina,* was presented at the Covent Garden Theatre in 1738. It was acted three times. On October 14, 1854, *Pericles,* with Gower omitted and the brothel scenes expurgated, was produced by Phelps, who took the title rôle. It was received with much enthusiasm, but it is impossible to read the laudatory accounts of Henry Morley and Douglas Jerrold without suspecting that some of their interest was due to the novelty of the production. An account of this performance is given in *The Henry Irving Shakespeare,* Vol. VIII, pp. 264, 265. On October 20, 1882, *Pericles* was presented at Munich, accompanied by music written for the occa-

---

[1] *Roscius Anglicanus,* p. 18. This was before the formation of Sir William Davenant's company, in which Betterton's great reputation was made.

sion. The genuine parts seem to have been highly successful. It has more recently been included in the repertory of Sir F. R. Benson's company at the **Shakespeare Memorial Theatre at Stratford-on-Avon.**

APPENDIX C

AUTHORSHIP OF THE PLAY

During the first century of the play's life, no doubt of its authenticity was expressed except by its exclusion from the First and Second Folios. Rowe included it in his edition of 1709, but it was rejected by Pope as spurious, and that view prevailed until Malone, in 1780, in his Supplement to Steevens' Shakespeare of 1778, argued that it was a genuine, though youthful, production of Shakespeare. Steevens at first dissented, but finally, in 1790, adopted the theory of a double authorship. With few exceptions, scholars have now agreed that *Pericles* is only partly the work of Shakespeare, and it is included among his later plays. This leaves three questions for discussion: 1. How much of it is attributable to Shakespeare? 2. Who wrote the rest? 3. Did Shakespeare's contribution precede or follow the work of the other author or authors?

1. The general opinion is that the largely or wholly Shakespearean part begins with Act III, Scene i, that is, that he is the author of the portion dealing with the fortunes of Marina. This is the conclusion to which Tennyson came, anticipating the editors by some years, and his reading of the parts he considered genuine seems to have carried conviction to his hearers. It is also the conclusion of Swinburne, who expresses the utmost enthusiasm for the portion he accepted. But there is still divergence of opinion as to whether Shakespeare had any hand in the first two acts, and whether he wrote all of the last three. Of course, those who hold that his original play on the story of Marina was later completed by another writer—a theory to be discussed presently—must

deny him any share in the drama before Marina appears. H. D. Sykes,[1] finding parallels to Wilkins rife in Acts I and II, would therefore insist that Shakespeare had no hand in them, while Frank Harris,[2] in a burst of enthusiasm over the speech beginning

See where she comes apparell'd like the spring

(I. i. 12)

concludes that the whole work is Shakespeare's. As a matter of fact, neither of these methods is admissible. If it be once granted, as Sykes maintains, that Shakespeare worked over another writer's play, nothing less than proof that every line of a certain part is the work of the other writer will suffice to prove that Shakespeare has not touched that part at all; while the fact that there are fine passages in the first two acts cannot prove that he wrote the absurdities of Act II, Scene v, for instance, which Steevens condemns so roundly. Coleridge once remarked that Shakespeare's share in the play could be recognized 'even to half a line,' but as he never recorded which half lines he meant, and as subsequent critics show no disposition to agree, it is safest to conclude merely that there are some passages, before the appearance of Marina, which are worthy of the master, but that there are many which are certainly unworthy of him. In the latter half of the play, there are two parts which challenge attention, the Gower choruses and the brothel scenes. It will be observed that the Gower choruses of Acts IV and V, with the exception of that before Act IV, Scene ii, are in pentameter instead of tetrameter, and it has been argued that Shakespeare wrote the five foot lines, but not the four foot: a clear distinction, which though it cannot

[1] *Sidelights on Shakespeare,* Stratford-upon-Avon, 1919, pp. 141-203.

[2] *The Women of Shakespeare,* London, 1911, pp. 231 ff.

be considered proved, has enough confirmation from the substance of the choruses to be probable. The brothel scenes are generally held to be by a second or even a third hand. The origin of this theory is a natural desire to believe that Shakespeare did not write scenes so repellent. But extreme measures would be necessary to take all the objectionable scenes out of Shakespeare, and a candid reading of the ones in this play will show that there is considerable restraint about them, as well as a definite purpose; the illustration of Marina's virtue by the blackness of her surroundings. There are, moreover, definitely Shakespearean touches in such quantity that it is rather the part of prejudice than of scholarship to deny his authorship of them. The only other portion whose authenticity is denied is the vision of Diana (V. i. 241-250). Fleay regarded it as spurious, like the vision in *Cymbeline,* Act V, Scene iv, and recent editors have quoted him with approval. But, whatever may be the reasons for rejecting the passage in *Cymbeline,* it is hard to see why they should be held to apply also to this. The episode cannot be interpolated, for it occurs in the sources and is certainly essential to the plot; and it is so far superior in technique to the average of the non-Shakespearean parts that there seem to be no good grounds for assigning it to the author of them. Even Sykes, an indefatigable searcher for the traces of Wilkins, can find little evidence of him in the rest of Acts III, IV, and V. Our conclusion, then, is that Shakespeare is responsible for occasional passages of the first two acts, and for practically all the rest of the play, excepting the tetrameter Gower choruses.

2. Setting aside, for the moment, the brothel scenes, there are two serious contestants for the authorship of the rest of the play: George Wilkins and Thomas Heywood. Wilkins, of whom practically nothing is

known, is certainly the author of a comedy entitled
The Miseries of Enforced Marriage (1607),[1] besides
collaborating with Day and Rowley in *The Travells
of Three English Brothers* (1607).[2] The prose works
that bear his name are: *The Three Miseries of Bar-
bary; Plague, Famine, Civil War* (1603); *Jests to
Make you Merrie; with the conjuring up of Cock
Watt the walking Spirit of Newgate,* written in col-
laboration with Dekker (1607); and, most important
for us, *The Painful Adventures of Pericles, Prince of
Tyre* (1608). A pamphlet entitled *Two Unnatural
Murders* (1605) and the play, *A Yorkshire Tragedy,*
published in 1608 with Shakespeare's name attached,
have been conjecturally ascribed to him,[3] as also some
part in *Law Tricks,*[4] published in 1608 under Day's
name, and in *Timon of Athens*[5] (1607-1608?). It will
be seen that he was a man of varied, if meagre, talents.
There can be no doubt of the close connection between
the novel and the play. The title-page of the former
announces it to be 'The true History of the Play of
Pericles,' and the similarities are continual and self-
evident. Delius[6] advanced the theory that Wilkins
had written the original play, which was revised by
Shakespeare, in 1608, whereupon Wilkins produced
his novel, which he calls, in the dedication, the
'poore infant of my braine.' It purported to be
founded on the play alone, but actually followed also
the reprint of Twine's novel in 1607. Delius held
that the phrase 'poore infant of my braine' was in-

---

[1] Reprinted in Hazlitt's *Dodsley*, Vol. IX.

[2] Published with Day's works by G. A. Bullen, 1881.

[3] H. D. Sykes, op. cit. pp. 77-98.

[4] Robert Boyle, *Transactions of the New Shakespeare
Society*, 1882, pp. 323-340.

[5] N. Delius, *Jahrbuch der Deutschen Shakespeare-
Gesellschaft*, 1867, pp. 335-361. This has little evidence to
justify it, and has received no subsequent support.

[6] *Jahrbuch*, 1868, pp. 175-204.

tended by Wilkins to refer to his origination of the
play; he adduced further evidence from a comparison
with *The Miseries of Enforced Marriage* and those
parts of *Timon* which he took to be Wilkins', finding
likenesses, in their common artistic mediocrity, in the
mixture of rhyme, blank verse and prose, and in the
technique of both prose and verse.   Fleay[1] stated
rather than proved metrical similarities looking to
the same conclusion, and his result was reinforced,
though his method was condemned, by Robert Boyle,[2]
who added similarities of language, of substance, and
of technique.   All this evidence is reviewed, with additions, by H. D. Sykes,[3] who stresses particularly
Wilkins' ellipses and his frequent use of verbal an-
tithesis.   He has extended the search to the other
works of Wilkins, certain and supposed, and has, indeed, collected an imposing number of parallel passages.   Moreover, he has made a detailed comparison
between the novel and the play, and come to the conclusion that the novel was written before the play, instead of following it.   He is obliged, however, by
the evidence of the title-page, to assume that Wilkins
delayed its publication until after the play, revised by
Shakespeare, had been produced.   For this he gives
no reason.   He cites the case of Pericles' harp-play-
ing (cf. III. v. 28 and n.), and maintains, besides
the greater inherent probability of an Elizabethan
play made from a novel than of a novel made from a
play, that the passages in common are actually parts
of the novel introduced by Wilkins into the play.
His arguments are plausible, but not overwhelming.
In general it may be said that the case for Wilkins
is founded, first on the connection between the novel

[1] *Transactions of the New Shakespeare Society*, 1874,
pp. 195-241.
[2] Op. cit.
[3] Op. cit. pp. 141-203.

and the play, and, second, on similarities, largely of language, with Wilkins' other works.

In 1908, D. L. Thomas[1] suggested as the first author of *Pericles* the prolific Thomas Heywood. Thomas attacks the theory of Delius and Boyle, without doing it perfect justice, perhaps, but in a way to show certain weaknesses in it: the fact, for instance, that verbal likenesses are somewhat unsatisfactory unless they accompany likenesses of dramatic technique, and that, to be convincing, the champions of Wilkins ought to show that *Pericles* is verbally more like his works than like those of any other contemporary playwright. Thomas' own argument is largely concerned with dramatic devices, and the larger questions of conception, style and technique. He also cites twenty-three of what he calls 'dictional parallels' between *Pericles* and plays of Heywood, but they are not striking, nor is the number large, considering that two dozen of Heywood's plays are left. The arguments from construction and treatment of incidents are more convincing, but, in the end, they go rather to prove that Heywood could have written *Pericles* than that he did. The question cannot be considered settled until other possibilities have been examined as exhaustively as Wilkins and Heywood, but, at present, the weight of evidence is still in favor of the former.

The brothel scenes are considered as a separate problem by those who regard them as non-Shakespearean. Fleay recognized their superiority to the parts which he assigned to Wilkins, and, to avoid the difficulty, suggested Rowley (with whom Wilkins had collaborated before) as their author. Walker had already suggested Dekker, *faute de mieux.* J. M.

---

[1] *Englische Studien,* 1908, pp. 210-239. The article has received the polite dissent of subsequent scholars.

Robertson[1] argues for Chapman, as a corollary to his thesis that Chapman wrote similar parts of *Measure for Measure*. But here, the result of the argument is rather possibility than probability. No real similarity with Dekker or Rowley has been brought forward, and the case for Chapman is merely inferred from other conjectural conclusions. Of course, if we admit the scenes to be Shakespeare's, the problem disappears.

3. We have already seen that Sykes believes *Pericles* to be a revision by Shakespeare of another's play. This was the view expressed by Steevens and by Coleridge, who did not name the original author, and it has received the support of many commentators since. A bolder theory, but one with many advocates, is that of Fleay, who believed that Shakespeare originally wrote *The Story of Marina*[2]—that is, the greater part of the last three acts, and then laid it aside, for some reason or other, when it was completed by Wilkins and Rowley. The source of this supposition seems to be a feeling that Shakespeare would have disdained to work over so dull a performance as that of the other author. But for him to have written these acts, whether intending them for the beginning and end, as A. H. Smyth believes,[3] or for the end alone, as they actually became, seems unlikely in the extreme. In either case, it means that Shakespeare deliberately chose a theme which did not readily admit of dramatic unity, and wrote a piece, too short for presentation, with the conclusion

---

[1] *The Shakespeare Canon*, London, 1923. Part II, pp. 165, 184, 186.

[2] This part of the play is printed as a whole by Fleay in the *Transactions of the New Shakespeare Society* for 1874, pp. 211-241. It is preceded (pp. 195-209) by a discussion of his reasons for believing it to be Shakespeare's original production.

[3] *Pericles and Apollonius*, Philadelphia, 1898, p. 68.

complete, and, therefore, as hard as possible for anyone to fill out. 'To a piece of work so preposterous,
in the strict sense of the word, so useless for theatrical
purposes, so unsuitable for publication, the history
of literature affords, I think, no parallel.[1] Surely
the natural explanation is the right one, and we have
here, as Coleridge conjectured,[2] an illustration of
'the way in which Shakespeare handled a piece he
had to refit for representation.'

[1] K. Deighton. Introduction to *Pericles, The Arden
Shakespeare.*
[2] H. C. Robinson's Diary, Dec. 23, 1810.

APPENDIX D

The text of the present volume is, by permission of the Oxford University Press, that of the Oxford Shakespeare, edited by the late W. J. Craig, except for the following deviations:

1. The stage directions are those of the First Quarto of 1609, necessary additional words being inserted in square brackets.

2. The punctuation has been altered in many places, and the following changes in spelling have been made: Troyan (Trojan), iwis (I wis), spoken (speken), wanion (wannion), porpoise (porpus), joust (just), curst (curs'd), Oh (O), murtherer (murderer), anything (any thing), forever (for ever), anyone (any one), wandlike-straight (wand-like straight), godlike (god-like), seafarer (sea-farer).

3. The following alterations of the text have been made after collation with the First Quarto, readings of the present edition preceding and those of Craig following the colon. Unless otherwise specified, the readings of this text are those of the First Quarto. F stands for the Third Folio.

I. i. 17	rac'd (Q racte): raz'd
I. i. 20	have: hath
I. i. 38	Here they: They here
I. i. 82	man: men
I. i. 113	off (F): of
I. ii. 100	grieve for them: grieve them
II. Gower 36	escapen'd: escapen
II. i. 6	my: me
II. i. 82	pray you: pray
II. i. 83	forbid 't: forbid
II. i. 84	And I: I
II. i. 87	all day: holidays
II. i. 139	it (Malone): 't

II. i. 142	have given: they have given
II. i. 144	father gave in his: father's gift in 's
II. i. 152	fortune's: fortunes
II. i. 162	waters: water
II. i. 164	them: it
II. i. 165	believe 't: believe it
II. i. 167	rupture: rapture
II. i. 168	building: biding
II. ii. 10	It 's: 'Tis
II. ii. 33	Qui: Quod
II. ii. 36	an: a
II. ii. 47	fortunes: fortune
II. iii. 12	my: by
II. iii. 26	shall: do
II. iii. 101	Here's: Here is
II. iii. 102	have heard: have often heard
II. iv. 13	justice: just
II. iv. 25	your: the
II. iv. 33	leave: leaves
II. iv. 38	know: know'st
II. iv. 41	Try: For
II. v. 19	nay, how: how
II. v. 37	Sir, my daughter: My daughter, **sir**
II. v. 83	I'll: I will
II. v. 89	my: or
II. v. 93	And then: Then
III. Gower 8	Are: E'er
III. Gower 60	seas-toss'd: sea-tost
III. i. 1	The: Then
III. i. 26	Vie (Steevens): Use
III. i. 45	and: an
III. ii. 10	Good morrow: Good morrow, **sir**
III. ii. 36	dwells: dwell
III. ii. 48	never: ne'er decay
III. ii. 49	What's: What is
III. ii. 50	Toss up: Toss
III. ii. 56	bottomed: bitumed
III. ii. 59	Wrench: Come, wrench
III. ii. 67	in: i'
III. ii. 69	drives: drive
III. ii. 80	a fire: fire
III. ii. 81	my: the
III. ii. 84	o'erpress'd: overpress'd
III. ii. 86	appliance: appliances
III. ii. 97	sets: set
III. ii. 103	Doth: Do

III. ii. 107	my gentle: gentle
III. iii. 6	shakes: shafts, haunt (2d Q): hurt
III. iii. 14	leaving: and leave
IV. Gower 23	needle: neeld
IV. Gower 47	carried: carry
IV. i. 17	doth: do
IV. i. 19	is a: is like a
IV. ii. 52	farther: further
IV. ii. 118	Ay, he; he: Ay; he
IV. iii. 50	Do: Doth
IV. iv. G. 1	long: longest
IV. v. 32	deeds: deed
V. i. 9	there is: there's
V. i. 10	I pray: I pray ye, him: them
V. i. 15	you: you, sir
V. i. 47	parts: ports
V. i. 61	inflict: afflict
V. i. 64	here's: here is
V. i. 66	present: presence
V. i. 103	You're: You are
V. i. 119	If I should: Should I
V. i. 122	lookest: look'st
V. i. 124	I will believe: I believe
V. i. 165	daughter: daughter's
V. i. 168	You: You'll, scorn: scorn to
V. i. 179	imposture: imposter
V. i. 188	Here's: Here is
V. i. 209	The: Thou 'rt, like: life
V. i. 215	th' art: thou art
V. i. 227	dote: doubt
V. i. 234	Music, my lord? I hear: My lord I hear *Music*
V. i. 248	Or perform: Perform
V. ii. 19	overboard: o'erboard
V. ii. 21	overjoy'd: o'erjoyed
V. ii. 32	spake: speak
V. ii. 41	sports: sport
V. ii. 69	and: I
V. ii. 100	punish: punish them
V. ii. 102	has: hath

APPENDIX E

1. The Greek Romances.

    Scriptores Erotici Græci, edited by G. A. Hirshig (Paris, 1856). It contains also the text of a Paris MS. of *Apollonius.* The Greek text is accompanied by a Latin translation.

    The Greek Romances of Heliodorus, Longus, and Achilles Tatius. An English translation by Rowland Smith (London, 1893).

    E. Rohde: *Der griechische Roman und seine Vorläufer* (Leipzig, 1900).

    S. L. Wolff: *Greek Romances in Elizabethan Fiction* (New York, 1912).

    J. S. Phillimore: the delightful article on *Greek Romances* in *English Literature and the Classics* (Oxford, 1912).

2. The Story of Apollonius.

    A. H. Smyth: *Pericles and Apollonius* (Philadelphia, MacCalla, 1898). This discusses the origin of the legend and the Latin MSS., deals exhaustively with the versions in different languages, and prints the *Gesta Romanorum* text. It also gives references to all the important literature.

3. The Latin Version.

    Alexander Riese: *Historia Apollonii Regis Tyrii* (Teubner, 1893).

4. Godfrey of Viterbo.

    Monumenta Germaniæ Historica, Band xxii (Hanover, 1872).

5. The *Gesta Romanorum.*

>   Edition by Oesterley (Berlin, 1872).
>   Translation by Hooper (London, 1894).

6. Gower.

>   Edition by G. C. Macaulay (Oxford, 1899-1902).
>   W. C. Hazlitt: *Shakespeare's Library,* Part I, Vol. IV, pp. 176-228 (London, 1875).

7. Twine.

>   W. C. Hazlitt: op. cit. pp. 229-334.

8. Wilkins' Novel.

>   Edition by Tycho Mommsen (Oldenburg, 1857).

9. Lillo.

>   Paul von Hofman-Wellenhof: *Shakespeare's 'Pericles' und George Lillo's 'Marina'* (Wien, 1885).

10. The Text.

>   Facsimile of Quarto 1. Edited by P. Z. Round (London, Pretorius, 1886).
>   Facsimile of Quarto 1. Edited by Sidney Lee (Oxford, 1905).
>   Facsimile of Quarto 2. Edited by P. Z. Round (London, Pretorius, 1886).
>   *The First Folio Shakespeare,* Vol. 13 (London, n.d.) reprints the text of Quarto 1.

11. The Authorship of the Play.

>   Nicolaus Delius: *Ueber Shakespeare's Pericles* (*Jahrbuch der Deutschen Shakespeare-Gesellschaft,* Vol. III, pp. 175-204).
>   Fleay: *On the Play of Pericles, The Birth and Life of Marina* (*Transactions of the New Shakespeare Society,* 1874, pp. 195-241).

R. Boyle: *On Wilkins' Share in the Play called Shakespeare's Pericles* (ibid. 1882, pp. 323-340).

D. L. Thomas: *On the Play Pericles* (*Englische Studien,* 1908, pp. 210-239).

H. D. Sykes: *Wilkins' and Shakespeare's Pericles, Prince of Tyre* (*Sidelights on Shakespeare,* Stratford-upon-Avon, 1919).

12. The Date of the Play.

T. S. Graves: *On the Date and Significance of Pericles* (*Modern Philology,* 1916, pp. 177-188).

13. Editions.

Variorum by Malone (London, 1821). An invaluable compendium of the commentators up to that time.

The Henry Irving Shakespeare, Vol. VIII, by P. Z. Round (London, n.d.). The introduction is very useful for the stage history of the play.

Shakspere's Werke, Vol. 7, by Nicolaus Delius (Eberfeld, 1864). This is the most conservative of the modern texts. It has notes in German, and large selections reprinted from Gower, Twine, and Wilkins.

The Cambridge Shakespeare, by W. A. Wright (London, 1893). There are brief notes, an exhaustive bibliography, and a full critical apparatus.

The Arden Shakespeare, by K. Deighton (London, 1907). This contains a brief but good critical apparatus.

INDEX OF WORDS GLOSSED

(Figures in full-faced type refer to page-numbers)

absolute: **53** (IV. Gower 31)
abuts against: **79** (V. i. 51)
act: **9** (I. ii. 18)
action: **41** (III. Gower 55)
address'd: **33** (II. iii. 94)
ador'd: **34** (II. iv. 11)
Æsculapius: **49** (III. ii. 111)
aid: **46** (III. ii. 35)
all: **53** (IV. Gower 34)
all perishen of man: **20** (II. Gower 35)
ambo: **39** (II. v. 91)
and: **43** (III. i. 45)
and though: **25** (II. i. 133)
Apollo: **48** (III. ii. 67)
aptly: **87** (V. ii. 5)
are: **40** (III. Gower 8)
are arms: **11** (I. ii. 74)
argentine: **86** (V. i. 251)
artificial feat: **80** (V. i. 72)
as: **3** (I. i. 16); **9** (I. ii. 3)
aspire: **15** (I. iv. 5)
at: **45** (III. i. 82)
at large: **79** (V. i. 62)
attend: **11** (I. ii. 70)
attribute: **64** (IV. iii. 18)
awkward: **81** (V. i. 94)

bases: **26** (II. i. 173)
bated one doit: **60** (IV. ii. 55)
be you thoughten: **73** (IV. vi. 119)
beadle: **24** (II. i. 100)
been: **32** (II. iii. 82)
beholding: **37** (II. v. 25); **86** (V. i. 224)
benison: **19** (II. Gower 10)
bent all offices: **38** (II. v. 48)
best: **33** (II. iii. 116)

better: **74** (IV. vi. 177)
bitumed: **44** (III. i. 72)
bless: **91** (V. iii. 69)
blurted: **65** (IV. iii. 34)
blush: **7** (I. i. 135)
bolins: **43** (III. i. 43)
bootless: **78** (V. i. 33)
boots it me: **9** (I. ii. 20)
bots: **25** (II. i. 128)
bourn: **66** (IV. iv. 4)
brace: **25** (II. i. 137)
braid: **5** (I. i. 93)
breathing: **33** (II. iii. 101)
but: **71** (IV. vi. 76)
but sea-room: **43** (III. i. 45)
by the syllable: **84** (V. i. 169)

can: **9** (I. ii. 18); **41** (III. Gower 36)
canvas-climber: **56** (IV. i. 61)
cates: **30** (II. iii. 29)
censure: **35** (II. iv. 34)
characters: **48** (III. ii. 67)
charge: **43** (III. i. 27)
chaste: **70** (IV. vi. 44)
cheapen: **69** (IV. vi. 10)
chequins: **59** (IV. ii. 28)
choleric fisting: **75** (IV. vi. 182)
cloudy billow: **43** (III. i. 46)
command: **74** (IV. vi. 177)
commend: **29** (II. ii. 49)
conceit: **42** (III. i. 16)
condolements: **26** (II. i. 163)
confound: **88** (V. ii. 14)
consist: **18** (I. iv. 83)
conversation: **19** (II. Gower 9)

convince: 13 (I. ii. 123)
cope: 73 (IV. vi. 136)
copp'd: 6 (I. i. 101)
corse: 47 (III. ii. 63)
countervail: 31 (II. iii. 56)
courses: 56 (IV. i. 38)
coystril: 75 (IV. vi. 181)
cross: 64 (IV. iii. 16)
crosses: 86 (V. i. 246)
curious: 3 (I. i. 16)
cut: 41 (III. Gower 45)

darks: 53 (IV. Gower 35)
dear: 75 (IV. vi. 195)
deep clerks she dumbs: 76 (V. Gower 5)
deliver'd: 83 (V. i. 162)
depart: 14 (I. iii. 18)
discover'd: 77 (V. Gower 24)
distain: 65 (IV. iii. 31)
distemperature: 78 (V. i. 27)
doit: 60 (IV. ii. 55)
dooms: 41 (III. Gower 32)
dote: 86 (V. i. 227)
doubt it: 12 (I. ii. 86)
drawn: 84 (V. i. 175)
dropping: 57 (IV. i. 62)
drouth: 40 (III. Gower 8)
drunk to: 64 (IV. iii. 11)

eaning time: 52 (III. iv. 6)
earnest: 60 (IV. ii. 49)
eche: 40 (III. Gower 13)
effectless: 79 (V. i. 53)
eftsoons: 87 (V. i. 256)
ember-eves: 1 (I. Gower 6)
endurance: 82 (V. i. 138)
entertain: 6 (I. i. 119)
entertainment: 60 (IV. ii. 60)
entrance: 31 (II. iii. 64)
entreasur'd: 48 (III. ii. 65)
environed with: 28 (II. ii. 36)
equivalent: 81 (V. i. 92)

et bonum quo antiquius, eo melius: 1 (I. Gower 10)
even: 43 (III. i. 27)
extremity out of act: 82 (V. i. 141)
eyne: 39 (III. Gower 5)

fact: 64 (IV. iii. 12)
fame: 40 (III. Gower 22)
favour: 55 (IV. i. 24)
fell: 41 (III. Gower 53)
fere: 1 (I. Gower 21)
fitment: 69 (IV. vi. 6)
flaw: 43 (III. i. 39)
for: 12 (I. ii. 92)
for going on: 4 (I. i. 40)
forbear: 35 (II. iv. 46)
fore: 40 (III. Gower 6)
frame: 2 (I. Gower 32)
full bent with sin: 20 (II. Gower 23)
full wanderingly: 50 (III. iii. 7)

give over: 59 (IV. ii. 30)
given: 53 (IV. Gower 35)
glad: 20 (II. Gower 38)
glad her presence: 3 (I. i. 9)
gloze: 6 (I. i. 110)
gone through: 60 (IV. ii. 47)
graceful marks: 54 (IV. Gower 36)
graff: 79 (V. i. 60)
green: 55 (IV. i. 14)
green-sickness: 69 (IV. vi. 14)
greets: 65 (IV. iii. 38)

half: 41 (III. Gower 45)
half-part: 58 (IV. i. 94)
haling: 56 (IV. i. 54)
happily: 18 (I. iv. 92)
harpy: 66 (IV. iii. 46)
has me: 69 (IV. vi. 7)
hatched: 59 (IV. ii. 37)

have, an wish but for 't: 66 (IV. iv. 2)

he: 88 (V. ii. 12)

heart and place: 53 (IV. Gower 10)

heaven: 1 (I. Gower 24)

heavy: 77 (V. Gower 22)

Hesperides: 3 (I. i. 27)

hight: 53 (IV. Gower 18)

his mortal vessel: 67 (IV. iv. 30)

holds his building: 26 (II. i. 168)

holy-ales: 1 (I. Gower 6)

how chance: 55 (IV. i. 22)

husbandry: 46 (III. ii. 20)

i' the justice of compare: 64 (IV. iii. 9)

if: 82 (V. i. 137)

if put upon you: 72 (IV. vi. 102)

in aught you would: 78 (V. i. 12)

in feather'd briefness: 88 (V. ii. 15)

in hac spe vivo: 28 (II. ii. 44)

indenture: 14 (I. iii. 9)

inflict: 79 (V. i. 61)

inkle: 76 (V. Gower 8)

inquire: 40 (III. Gower 22)

intend: 13 (I. ii. 116)

is it: 85 (V. i. 211)

is mortal: 49 (III. ii. 110)

it: 55 (IV. i. 26)

iwis: 19 (II. Gower 2)

jetted: 16 (I. iv. 26)

joy: 9 (I. ii. 9)

justify: 85 (V. i. 219)

kept: 25 (II. i. 140)

labour: 27 (II. ii. 15)

lading: 10 (I. ii. 49)

length: 8 (I. i. 168)

level: 33 (II. iii. 114)

levy: 38 (II. v. 52)

lien: 48 (III. ii. 85)

like: 35 (II. iv. 36)

litigious: 50 (III. iii. 3)

longs: 20 (II. Gower 40)

loud music: 33 (II. iii. 97)

lown: 69 (IV. vi. 19)

Lucina: 3 (I. i. 8)

lux tua vita mihi: 27 (II. ii. 21)

made up: 26 (II. i. 161)

makes: 91 (V. iii. 74)

malkin: 65 (IV. iii. 34)

malleable: 74 (IV. vi. 157)

manage: 71 (IV. vi. 70)

marry, come up: 74 (IV. vi. 164)

mart: 58 (IV. ii. 5)

mask'd Neptune: 51 (III. iii. 36)

may men approve: 22 (II. i. 56)

me pompæ provexit apex: 28 (II. ii. 30)

mean: 29 (II. ii. 59)

mere: 63 (IV. ii. 134)

minding: 34 (II. iv. 3)

more, if might: 77 (V. Gower 23)

move: 32 (II. iii. 71)

my father gave: 25 (II. i. 144)

neeld: 76 (V. Gower 5)

neglection: 50 (III. iii. 20)

nicely: 54 (IV. i. 6)

night-bird: 53 (IV. Gower 26)

nill: 41 (III. Gower 55)

nips: 86 (V. i. 235)

nousle: 16 (I. iv. 42)

nursing: 45 (III. i 82)

o'erpress'd: 48 (III. ii. 84)

of: 55 (IV. i. 24)

of all say'd yet: 4 (I. i. 59)

offence: **12** (I. ii. 92)
offend: **71** (IV. vi. 76)
on: **29** (II. ii. 54); **32** (II. iii. 92)
open: **65** (IV. iii. 23)
or: **86** (V. i. 248)
orbs: **13** (I. ii. 122)
ostent: **10** (I. ii. 25)
overcome: **17** (I. iv. 70)

paced: **71** (IV. vi. 68)
pain: **47** (III. ii. 46)
pained'st: **75** (IV. vi. 178)
Paphos: **53** (IV. Gower 32)
partakes: **8** (I. i. 152)
parted: **90** (V. iii. 38)
parts: **72** (IV. vi. 89)
pay your bounties: **25** (II. i. 153)
pelf: **20** (II. Gower 35)
peremptory: **38** (II. v. 73)
perfect: **48** (III. ii. 67); **85** (V. i. 208)
physic: **46** (III. ii. 32)
piece of virtue: **73** (IV. vi. 122)
Pilch: **21** (II. i. 12)
piu por dulzura que por fuerza: **28** (II. ii. 27)
place: **53** (IV. Gower 10)
pooped: **59** (IV. ii. 25)
poor worm: **6** (I. i. 102)
portage: **43** (III. i. 35)
portly: **17** (I. iv. 61)
prefer: **27** (II. ii. 17)
pregnant: **54** (IV. Gower 44)
prest: **54** (IV. Gower 45)
Priapus: **69** (IV. vi. 4)
principals: **46** (III. ii. 16)
prorogue: **78** (V. i. 26)
purchase: **1** (I. Gower 9)
put off: **7** (I. i. 140)

questionless: **79** (V. i. 45)
qui me alit me extinguit: **28** (II. ii. 33)

quick: **55** (IV. i. 27)
quirks: **69** (IV. vi. 8)
quit: **43** (III. i. 35)

rac'd: **3** (I. i. 17)
raw: **60** (IV. ii. 60)
receiv'd: **2** (I. i. 1)
records: **53** (IV. Gower 27)
recovered: **89** (V. iii. 24)
relation: **82** (V. i. 125)
relish'd: **38** (II. v. 60)
report: **70** (IV. vi. 43)
resolve: **38** (III. v. 68)
respect: **51** (IV. iii. 33)
return them: **27** (II. ii. 4)
riding: **88** (V. iii. 11)
rupture: **26** (II. i. 167)
rust: **29** (II. ii. 54)

sense: **5** (I. i. 81)
shine: **13** (I. ii. 124)
should: **2** (I. Gower 28); **85** (V. i. 217)
sic spectanda fides: **28** (II. ii. 38)
sight: **78** (V. i. 33)
sign: **62** (IV. ii. 126)
silk: **76** (V. Gower 8)
sisters: **76** (V. Gower 7)
sleided: **53** (IV. Gower 21)
smooth: **11** (I. ii. 78)
so this was well ask'd: **33** (II. iii. 99)
softly: **56** (IV. i. 48)
some of worth: **77** (V. i. 9)
sources: **65** (IV. iii. 28)
spite: **26** (II. i. 167)
standing-bowl: **31** (II. iii. 65)
stay: **27** (II. ii. 3)
stead: **40** (III. Gower 21)
steerage: **67** (IV. iv. 19)
still: **2** (I. Gower 36)
stint: **68** (IV. iv. 42)
stomach: **55** (IV. i. 28)
striv'd: **76** (V. Gower 16)
strongest: **35** (II. iv. 34)

subtilty: **37** (II. v. 44)
succeed: **12** (I. ii. 83)
suddenly: **44** (III. i. 70)
suit: **87** (V. i. 262)
supposing: **77** (V. Gower 21)

take I: **35** (II. iv. 43)
target: **25** (II. i. 147)
targets: **7** (I. i. 140)
telling your haste: **8** (I. i. 161)
Tellus: **55** (IV. i. 13)
tempest: **67** (IV. iv. 30)
thankful doom: **88** (V. ii. 20)
that: **76** (V. Gower 9); **90** (V. iii. 42)
that bears recovery's name: **79** (V. i. 54)
the common body: **50** (III. iii. 21)
the good: **19** (II. Gower 9)
the time of day: **65** (IV. iii. 35)
thee: **13** (I. ii. 116)
Thetis: **67** (IV. iv. 39)
think his pilot thought: **66** (IV. iv. 18)
this ornament: **91** (V. iii. 73)
thorough: **65** (IV. iii. 35)
thy: **26** (II. i. 169); **44** (III. i. 77)
time: **13** (I. ii. 123)
tire: **46** (III. ii. 22)
to: **36** (II. iv. 54); **65** (IV. iii. 25); **82** (V. i. 126)
to all reports: **55** (IV. i. 35)
to owe: **82** (V. i. 118)
to the life: **86** (V. i. 247)
to-bless: **69** (IV. vi. 23)
to-morrow: **33** (II. iii. 116)
to-night: **48** (III. ii. 77)
told: **41** (III. Gower 57)
told not: **2** (I. Gower 38)
touchstone: **28** (II. ii. 37)

triumph: **29** (II. ii. 53)
Troyan horse: **18** (I. iv. 93)
Tyre: **44** (III. i. 77)

unlaid ope: **12** (I. ii. 89)
upon: **50** (III. iii. 5)
us'd: **9** (I. ii. 3)
usurp: **48** (III. ii. 82)

vail: **53** (IV. Gower 29)
vails: **26** (II. i. 163)
Valdes: **58** (IV. i. 96)
vestal livery: **52** (III. iv. 10)

wages not: **59** (IV. ii. 34)
warrant: **63** (IV. ii. 141); **82** (V. i. 136)
waste: **66** (IV. iv. 1)
waters: **26** (II. i. 162)
we: **43** (III. i. 24)
well favour'd: **57** (IV. i. 85)
well-a-near: **41** (III. Gower 51)
whereas: **17** (I. iv. 70)
which: **63** (IV. ii. 141)
whirring: **55** (IV. i. 20)
why: **14** (I. iii. 17)
will: **33** (II. iii. 95)
with a wanion: **21** (II. i. 17)
with rosemary and bays: **74** (IV. vi. 165)
woo'd: **84** (V. i. 174)
would: **6** (I. i. 100); **75** (IV. vi. 195)
writ: **19** (II. Gower 12)

yield: **36** (II. iv. 54)
you: **35** (II. iv. 25); **43** (III. i. 26); **89** (V. iii. 26)
your date expire: **52** (III. iv. 14)
yravished: **41** (III. Gower 35)
yslacked hath the rout: **39** (III. Gower 1)